Modern Poetry in Translation
Series Three, Number 4

Between the Languages

Edited by David and Helen Constantine

MODERN POETRY IN TRANSLATION

Modern Poetry in Translation
No. 4, Series Three
© Modern Poetry in Translation 2005 and contributors
ISBN 0-9545367-4-6
ISSN 0969-3572

Printed and bound in Great Britain by Short Run Press, Exeter

Editors: David and Helen Constantine
Reviews Editor: Josephine Balmer
Administrator: Deborah de Kock

Submissions should be sent in hard copy with return postage to David and Helen Constantine, Queen's College, Oxford, OX1 4AW, UK. Unless agreed in advance, submissions by email will not be considered. Translators are themselves responsible for obtaining any necessary permissions and copyright clearance.

Founding Editors: Ted Hughes and Daniel Weissbort

Subscription Rates: (including postage)

	UK	Overseas
Single Issue	£11	£13 / US$ 24
One year subscription (2 issues, surface mail)	£22	£26 / US$ 48
Two year subscription (4 issues, surface mail)	£40	£48 / US$ 88

To subscribe please use the subscription form at the back of the magazine. Discounts available.

To pay by credit card please visit www.mptmagazine.com

Modern Poetry in Translation is represented in UK by Central Books
99 Wallis Road, London, E9 5LN

For orders: tel +44 (0) 845 458 9910 Fax +44 (0) 845 458 9912 or visit www.mptmagazine.com

Contents

1   Editorial

5   **Kapka Kassabova** Polyglot Peregrinations

14 **Amarjit Chandan** Inhabiting two Planets

19 **Itsik Manger** Four Poems, with three translations and a literal version, introduced by Helen Beer

36 **Michael Hamburger** Afterthoughts on the Mug's Game

59 **Mary-Ann Constantine** 'To let in the light': Gwyneth Lewis's Poetry of Transition.

66 **Gwyneth Lewis** Two Poems, translated by Mary-Ann Constantine and the author

70 **Choman Hardi** 'Switching Languages: a Hindrance or an Opportunity?'

73 **Poet to Poet** The Scotland-China Project. Introduction by Polly Clark

92 **Antonella Anedda** Five Poems, translated by Jamie McKendrick

100 **Dimitris Tsaloumas** Four Poems, translated, with an introduction, by Helen Constantine

108 Extracts from **Mourid Barghouti**'s *Midnight*, translated by Radwa Ashour

124 'Dear Fahimeh', translated by Hubert Moore and Nasrin Parvaz

127 Extracts from **Sherko Bekes**'s *The Valley of Butterfly*, translated by Choman Hardi

155 **Ingeborg Bachmann** Ten Poems, translated by Patrick Drysdale and Mike Lyons, with an introduction by Karen Leeder

169 **Rimbaud** Versions of Three Poems, by Martin Bennett

172 **Bertolt Brecht** Ten Poems of Exile, translated by Timothy Adès

184 **Ivan Radoev** Three Poems, translated by Kapka Kassabova

188 **Anthony Rudolf** 'Any Ideas?' Calling all Poetry Detectives

194 **Josephine Balmer** A Note on Reviewing Translation

Reviews

197 Olivier Burckhardt on Claire Malroux's *Birds and Bison*, translated by Marilyn Hacker

200 **Sasha Dugdale** on Ileana Mălăncioiu's, *After the Raising of Lazarus,* translated by Eiléan Ní Chuilleanáin

205 Shorter Reviews and Further Books Received

207 Notes on Contributors

211 MPT Back Issues

Editorial

The novelist and essayist Elias Canetti was born and lived the first six years of his life in Ruschuk, Bulgaria, on the Lower Danube. There – so he remembers in his autobiography *Die gerettete Zunge* ('The tongue set free') – you might hear seven or eight languages being spoken on the streets around you. In his own family three were current: Spanish in a form that had scarcely developed since the late fifteenth century when the Sephardic Jews were driven from their homes in the Iberian Peninsula; German, but only between the mother and father, especially when they wished to exclude the children from understanding; and Bulgarian, spoken by the half dozen young girls who were always in the household as servants. These girls told him horror stories – of vampires and werewolves – in Bulgarian, terrifying him and themselves in so doing. In 1911 the family emigrated to Manchester, Canetti learned English. Two years later he was in Vienna, and got the language he would be a writer in: German. He lost all his Bulgarian. The horror stories, by some mysterious movement of the psyche, as though they insisted on being remembered, translated themselves, in his memory, into German. They jumped ship, transferred to another carrier, in order to survive.

People with English as their mother tongue generally feel well-off, often smugly so. The advantages are indeed great; but they bring with them an almost equal risk of laziness, arrogance and insularity. And thinking about Canetti, and reading some of the contributions in this issue of *MPT*, even those native speakers of English who have acquired another tongue or two, may well feel rather humbled.

But a thorough ability in more than one language may itself be a troubled and problematic state. Often it is only achieved by force of circumstances, perhaps of a murderous kind: the driving and scattering abroad, the loss of a mother tongue among foreigners. One reason for the many suicides among writers in exile, German writers for example between 1933 and 1945, is the loss of speech and the loss of a readership of native speakers. Brecht, a survivor, in exile in America, noted in his journal that he was beginning to lose some German words – whilst wilfully, deliberately, not replacing them with English. Hölderlin was certain that all poets must, literally or figuratively, by travel or translation, go abroad; but warned against too long a stay there, for fear of losing the tongue and the self with it.

Language expresses and determines identity perhaps in equal measure. Anyone with any fluency in a foreign tongue knows the feeling of taking on another persona in the crossing over. That is not to suggest an insincerity. The bodily gestures of languages, their ways of being in the world, vary greatly; and the speakers, crossing over, shift more or less with their speech. This question of language and identity touches poetry closely. Thomas Hardy described his poems as 'personative' or 'impersonative'; even – he implied – those that seemed most to be in the author's own voice. There is nothing suspect or disreputable in assuming personae; each is a mask through which a possible human being speaks. The chief moral drive of poetry lies precisely in this sympathizing with ways of being human, with points of view and possibilities quite other than those inhabited by the writer in his or her own circumscribed biographical self. It is a waiving or subordinating of personal identity, the better to understand others.

At the same time, there has to be a centre, something that holds, a watchful place. Poems come about through an act of deliberate shaping, not through dissolution and letting go. A poet between or among the languages, already, as poet, entertaining the different identities that come with the poetic undertaking and compounding these with the identity adopted in the taking on of a new language, any such writer must be acutely attentive to the peculiar centre from which a poem issues. But the writers represented here do not need telling that.

English seems to prove the truth of the first half of Matthew 25:29 'Unto every one that hath shall be given, and he shall have in abundance'; and the languages struggling for survival around English must often feel they exemplify the rest: 'but from him that hath not shall be taken away even that which he hath'. We must work for something better, a productive struggle and in it an assertion and strengthening of identities. But what benefits come to English when writers settle in it and begin to import what they love and honour from the language they were born in! Michael Hamburger has for many years conducted German poets into English; Kapka Kassabova and Choman Hardi, each with a book of poems in English to her name, are beginning to fetch in works from the mother tongue. Writers in languages less world-wide than English rightly want to be known in it. And English, for its own lively development, has an equal interest in knowing them. The whole ambition of this magazine is to further that humane exchange.

David and Helen Constantine
October 2005

Contributions for the next issue of MPT

The next issue of *MPT*, Third Series, Number 5, will be called *Transgressions*. We are looking for translations and original poems that explore the possibilities in that title. We have in mind such things as the crossing of the borders of sex, gender, family, creed, race or nation – any such crossings that might be risky, unusual, un-conventional, and which might in the past have invited censure and punishment, or might do so still. Translation has often been a sort of smuggling, a dealing in the illegal or the illicit, and has been dangerous (and productive) in that sense. We invite contributions!

Deadline for submissions to the editors is 1 March 2006.

Submissions should be sent in hard copy with return postage to David and Helen Constantine, Queen's College, Oxford, OX1 4AW, UK. Unless agreed in advance, submissions by email will not be considered. Translators are themselves responsible for obtaining any necessary permissions and copyright clearance.

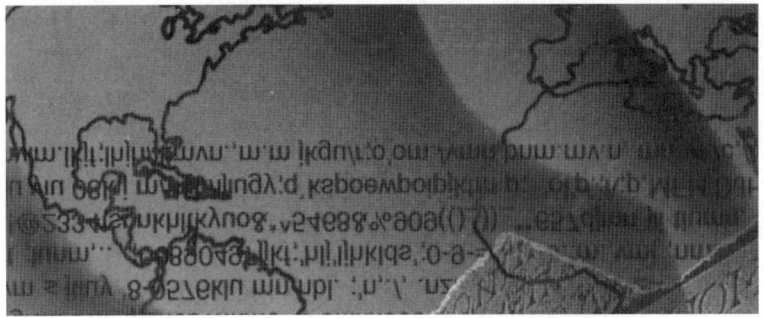

Kapka Kassabova
Polyglot Peregrinations

A foreign language is a paradoxical escape: it takes you out of yourself, but also back into yourself to places you didn't know existed. To translate is to travel this unpredictable landscape. To live between languages, as in my case, is to be constantly moving over untrodden territory, negotiating internal and external boundaries of identity and meaning. I was born an escapist and a traveller, which is why I was gripped from the moment my Russian teacher wrote on the blackboard a funny-looking sentence in Cyrillic, then turned her bespectacled face to the class and said: 'Today, we are going to learn Russian.'

I was eight. The year was 1981, the place Sofia. Leonid Brezhnev, the last serious Soviet dictator, died soon after. My Russian teacher wept into her black shawl while we stood freezing in the school courtyard, listening to records of Soviet army songs. By then, I understood the songs. I also understood, with a child's instinct, that something was wrong with us, with these songs blaring out of megaphones, with the way we *had* to understand them. So, as an unconscious act of protest, I tried to be bad at Russian. I gave idiotic answers in class, infuriating the poor teacher. Being an idiot was unrewarding, but I persevered. But it wasn't to be. One day I found myself entertaining my little sister with a slide-show of Russian stories. I had to translate as well as I could for her benefit. My mother came in at one point, and praised me for my translation. I was secretly chuffed. I kept up my slide-shows, ostensibly for my sister. I started looking up Russian words in the dictionary, and that is how I stopped wanting to be bad at Russian – being good at it was much more fun. Around that time, I started writing poetry in Bulgarian – about railway stations and going away. I also read *Evgeni Onegin* in a bilingual edition, and was transfixed by the miracle of sustained rhyming translation. Gradually, books became the centre of my world. I stopped showing my sister slide-shows because I was too busy reading. It was a way of forgetting what was wrong with us, and travelling to other worlds in the only possible way.

When it was time to choose a secondary school, I applied for the English school. But my entrance exam results weren't good enough, and I only just made it into the French school. Bulgaria has a tradition of bilingual schools where subjects like chemistry, biology and history are taught by bilingual teachers. The first day at the Lycée Français, our teacher Madame Lambreva warned us in Bulgarian that from now on only French was to be spoken. When we feebly protested that we didn't speak any yet, she said: 'That's exactly why' and continued in French for the rest of the day. We were petrified. It was too much for the girl sitting next to me – first she started sobbing quietly, then crapped herself. Her mother had to come and take her away.

We were given one hundred new words per day. I went home and wrote down each word a hundred times, with the religious fervour of a convert. It almost didn't matter what language I was learning – it was foreign, it wasn't Russian, and that was enough. French took me out of my familiar self, and that surely meant it would also take me out of all that was wrong with us. We sang songs like 'La Normandie' and 'La Marseillaise' whose geography was a mystery – Normandy,

Marseille, those were mythical places, like the Underworld. We had marathon dictations in class packed with tricky-to-spell words like *inouïes*, 'unheard of': negative, feminine, plural, and triple vowel. Our French teachers, Mme Musaud and Monsieur Neuilly, were relaxed and surprisingly caring. Once, I drew the Eiffel Tower in a drawing class. Mme Musaud said 'That's a nice drawing. Have you been there?' I was mortified. Some of the kids' parents were diplomats and they had lived in countries like Algeria, Libya, or even France. But not me. When Monsieur Neuilly left, he gave me his address in France and I wretchedly copied it in my address book. He was as good as dead to me now. France was an idea, not a real place. Only its language was real, and I clung to it as if to a secret money-belt.

By the end of the first year, I spoke fluent French and read Sartre and Camus. In my second year, I translated Baudelaire into Bulgarian while stuck in hospital with an auto-immune disease. I could discuss in French the phosphate resources of the Balkan region, molecules with triple valence, and existentialism. Somehow, this was going to save me. I already knew, implicitly, that when you are a second-class nation, learning the language of first-class nations is the closest you can get to a ticket. The Iron Curtain was like the Styx. Poor as we were, perhaps we could pay our way with language units. Now my class-mates talked about studying medicine or law in France after school. Medicine and law scared me witless, but maybe that's what it took to get to France? Then, one day, the Berlin Wall fell. Bulgaria had a coup. The world as we knew it collapsed and anything was possible. I was sixteen.

My father went to Essex, England, as a research fellow for two years. The family followed. I found myself at Colchester Sixth Form College with a late 80s East European hair-style, the usual torments of adolescence, and rudimentary English. You see, I never thought I might need English. I had prepared for France. In class, my English teacher Joe Sheerin talked about *Waiting for Godot*. I had seen it three times, in Bulgarian.

'It's a funny play, isn't it,' he tried to involve the class. They chewed gum and couldn't give a shit.

'It's not funny,' I ventured for the first time, blushing deeply, 'it's sad, very sad.' Some kids sniggered. Joe Sheerin turned to me with blue eyes full of wonder, and said:

'Thank you. You've obviously seen the play. You see, in English, funny has two meanings. It also means strange. It's a funny language, English.'

And he smiled with all the kindness I needed to rescue me from disappearing into the black hole of English. When I wrote my first essay, full of grammatical mistakes, inventive spelling and semantic horrors, Joe Sheerin asked me if I wrote poetry. He suggested I translate some poems and show them to him. He was a poet himself; only a poet could have thrown me the life-belt of encouragement I needed in order to swim in the deep, cold currents of my new language. I was almost ready to try writing in English, when our UK visas expired and we had to go back to Sofia to wait for new ones. I was accepted by Leeds University, my father was offered a permanent job in England – but we needed the visas.

Those were dark times in Sofia: poverty, unemployment, power cuts, water cuts, shortages, mass immigration, and disillusion. My mother was diagnosed with a tumour and had to have a hysterectomy. In the hospital, they had no sheets – only newspapers. I had a bladder infection, then stopped eating as an act of protest – against what, I didn't know. My father went grey overnight. My sister was re-learning to be Bulgarian after two years in English schools. My boyfriend from England came to visit in the darkest winter of our family, and heroically fought through blizzards to buy Christmas cards for England. We waited ten interminable months for word from the Home Office. Bored and depressed, I enrolled in an intensive Spanish course. One more language couldn't hurt, besides I had always liked the husky sounds of Spanish.

For a month, I sat in a classroom and conjugated Spanish verbs in a sort of incantatory trance. Yo me voy, tu te vas, el se

va, nosotros nos vamos, nosotros nos vamos, nosotros nos vamos
... The world was out there, and I wanted to go and practise my languages. All I needed was a stamp in my passport.

The Home Office sent us three visas – minus mine. I had turned 18, no longer a 'dependent family member'. Fortunately, my parents had decided to have a back-up option and my father had applied for a lectureship in New Zealand. We became New Zealand residents before we even arrived in Dunedin some months later, thin and pallid from stress and passport complications. On our first supermarket trip, my father bought twenty-five cartons of juice – every available variety in the supermarket – and arranged them in neat rows in the kitchen with a madman's grin.

But supermarket thrills aside, Dunedin at the time struck me as Calvinist, provincial, and distinctly untropical. They worshipped someone called Robbie Burns who was apparently Scottish, and had a strange way of speaking: instead of saying pen, they said pin; they said bid for bed, and fush and chups for fish and chips. There were no other Bulgarians in town, definitely no French, and few Europeans. It was Colchester all over again, except this time my boyfriend was far away, and worst of all – my English had lapsed. I made no difference between long and short vowels, so that when I said 'shits', I really meant 'sheets'. Fortunately, the people of Dunedin were more polite than the kids in Joe Sheerin's class. I wanted to study English literature but couldn't muster the confidence, so I enrolled with French, Russian, and linguistics – my comfort zone.

I was a published poet in Bulgaria by now, and still thought, dreamt and wrote in Bulgarian. But as links with Bulgaria and England began to fade, it dawned on me that this was permanent, that my life from now on was the life of a migrant in an English-speaking country at the end of the world. France looked more out of reach than ever. I had to stop writing in Bulgarian. I had to start writing in English, translating wasn't good enough anymore, it was like second-hand writing, and I was as ever sensitive to notions of second hand and second class. If someone else (Joseph Conrad) had done it at the age of 19, so could I. But I wanted it to happen overnight. I wanted to start writing in a literary tradition that I didn't know, with a fluency I didn't even have in speech yet. In my haste, I became stuck between two languages. In my writing, I had let go of Bulgarian, but I couldn't go anywhere in English. I became speechless.

I entered the transitional muteness of the immigrant Eva Hoffman conjures in *Lost in Translation*: a muteness of the mind. If you can't formulate complex thoughts and images in *some* language, you become emptied of complex thoughts and images. You stop being yourself and enter a state of non-being, of invisibility. I was used to writing in Bulgarian like living in a well-appointed house: padding on soft carpets, muting the lights, glimpsing fantastical landscapes from the windows, conversing with the portraits of my ancestors on the walls, browsing the endless library. I was used to bringing the furniture of foreign languages into that house too – there was always room for more. But I had never tried writing poetry or fiction in another language – a completely different business from speaking well or simply conveying meaning, or even translating. Now that I tried, I found myself stranded in a mental no man's land, with no shelter in sight and no familiar landmarks. Who were my ancestors? Who were my contemporaries? All I knew of English literature were the novels of Jack London, Ray Bradbury, and Harriet Beecher Stowe, and some *Hamlet* – all in Bulgarian translation. Where did I begin? Whom did I ask? I was studying French literature, after all – Sartre and Camus, my old friends. But they couldn't help me now that I was in the thick of being and nothingness.

Instead of being yet another foreign language for me, English became my first non-language. And because my sense of self came from my articulateness, I lost my very sense of self. I underwent an identity meltdown. Of course at the time I blamed it on Dunedin. But while I was miserable in New

Zealand, I hated Bulgaria and detested Britain for what it had done to us. There was no place in the world where I wanted to be – because without language there is no self, and without self there is no perception, and therefore no place for you in the world. In other words, I wanted to die.

I became a professional anorexic, scratched my wrists, wrote emotionally hysterical poems in English with lots of blood, and thought about quick ways to die, since self-starvation was clearly going to take time. But my parents had wrestled the monster of bureaucracy and the spectre of ill fortune to bring us here, and were now saving every penny to educate us and give us nice bedrooms and twenty-five varieties of fruit juice. I couldn't. Then one day, in the swimming pool where I went to burn off the fat I didn't have, I met a psychiatrist. He was clearly experienced because as we parted, he told me where to look for him if I needed to. He became my Joe Sheerin and my first friend: for a year, he gave me Prozac, his own wild poems, and books to read, among which were Sylvia Plath's poetry and *The Bell Jar*. By the end of the year, I was recovering: not just because Sylvia Plath could write about the way I felt in my psycho-linguistic bell-jar, but because I had started actually reading English literature. I had been given entry into the literary culture into which I so desperately wanted to read and write myself, so that I could exist once again. I was also meeting local writers, and even some French people to practise my French with. New Zealand stopped being a wasteland for me around the same time I found a tongue to be myself in – or at least to be someone.

In the meantime, I travelled to Tahiti on a one-month scholarship. There, I discovered that I was French. The Tahitians simply didn't believe that I was Bulgarian and had never been to France – I had the accent of 'métropole'. I was confused. I didn't want to be French – after all, I was writing in English now, and I had a Kiwi passport. France had never given me anything. But language has its own agenda. It is a giver and taker of identity sometimes on its own terms. Even now, when I fully inhabit English, and couldn't write in any other language, I cannot control my inflection which is a collection of accents. My poetry gets reviewed together with East European poets in translation. Yet when I met East European poets at the Dublin Writers' Festival last year and tried to find common ground, I couldn't – we didn't share a language or even a culture. To them I was an English-language writer. In Britain, people think I am French, but never a New Zealander or a Bulgarian. When I meet travelling Kiwis, they are perplexed when I insist I too am from New Zealand – I never learnt to say fush and chups. The only language in which I can pass off as a local is Bulgarian. But when I tried writing in Bulgarian once, I found myself regressing to the level of my sixteen-year-old self. When I go to Bulgaria now, exactly half a lifetime after I left, I feel like a foreigner. When I go to France, I queue up with my two passports and rusty French in the 'other' queue, still somehow second class, vaguely unclean.

Even now, with six published books in English (and the occasional translation into Bulgarian), my yearning for the language house I used to inhabit persists. Not for the Bulgarian language itself, but for the comfort of that residence. I have to accept that no matter how much I read, how many rare English words I know, and how many books I write in English, I will never live in such comfort again. The leather-bound volumes of Wordsworth and Tennyson will never be mine. They are borrowed, along with the writing desk, the UK visa, and the New Zealand passport. Walter Benjamin said that childhood is the source of all sorrow. It is also the source of all other profound experience, which is why inhabiting the ancestral house of language begins with childhood, with first memories and first picture books, with learning nursery rhymes and songs, and absorbing the moods of language while you are still a semi-conscious sponge. You cannot 'learn' nursery rhymes as an adult any more than you can learn memories, even though you can learn Shakespeare – and a writer's adventure with words starts not with Shakespeare, but with doggerel and lullabies, with slide-shows of fairy tales, with the deepest, pre-language memory of a certain smell of damp leaves. I write in English, but my memory of those damp autumn leaves is in Bulgarian. This is why I could only ever be a tenant in the English language house. This is also why I am geographically restless, searching for some kind of surrogate home that clearly doesn't exist.

This year, I found myself at a festival of Latin-American poetry in Vienna. I recited my poems in Spanish translation, with the Argentine accent I'd acquired on my travels to Buenos Aires. A German poet read my poems in German translation. The original English poems didn't get an airing. After the reading, an Austrian poet came up to chat in French. A Bulgarian expat introduced herself in Bulgarian. The Latin American community shouted in their various accents. An Argentine poet congratulated me on my Argentine pronunciation, and swore she had heard my poem at a festival in Colombia last year. An American expat spoke English with an English expat. Splinters of Austrian German flew around us. For a moment, caught up in this Babylonian cacophony, tuning in and out of meanings, I couldn't remember which language was supposed to be 'mine'. And yet, I wasn't confused by this. It was a happy moment of escape from the tyranny of a 'master' language. For once, I didn't have to prove myself, I didn't have to worry about being a native speaker, a foreigner, or a thing in between, about not remembering how to pronounce a certain word and betraying myself as being a tenant rather than a home-owner. It was a moment of polyphonic peace, like listening to the chanting of Gregorian monks.

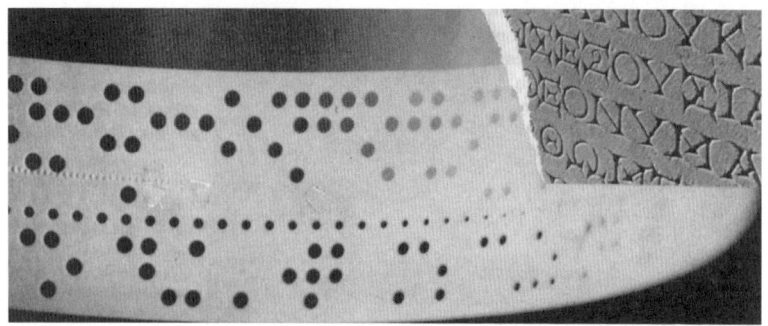

Amarjit Chandan
Inhabiting two planets

I

The history of the unequal relationship between English and Punjabi goes back to the early nineteenth century, when William Carey, a shoe-maker turned Baptist, published a ninety-nine-page *Grammar of the Punjabi Language* in 1812 in Calcutta, then the capital of British India. In 1849 the East India Company's army occupied the sovereign state of the Punjab, the land of my ancestors. The Punjab came under the control of the British Crown government in 1858. Seven years earlier John Newton of the Ludhiana Christian Mission in eastern Punjab had published the first-ever Punjabi translation of *The New Testament*, entitled *Anjeel* (after the French – évangile), along with a new *Grammar of the Punjabi Language*. The three-pronged process of politics, religion and linguistics was in full swing, though the African formula of the Bible and the Land had not been charted exactly in India. The religious conversion was negligible and the linguistic one was enormous. The British left India in 1947, dismembering the Punjab, but English still rules there; so much so that the Punjabi syntax, now mirroring the English sentence structure, is changed forever.

With the steam locomotive came the colonial locomotive that was full of a new class of western-oriented Indian gentlemen, better known as *baboos*. Careerists – the offspring of Lord Macaulay's agenda of educating Indians to craft a nation of petty clerks – soon learnt to take pride in attaining glibness in English. Lord Macaulay had said that 'a single shelf of a good European library is worth the whole native literature of India'. In that belief, Indian schoolchildren of future generations were made to cram Shakespeare's sonnet 'Let me not to the marriage of true minds . . .', Wordsworth's 'Daffodils' and Shelley's 'Ozymandias', ignoring their own linguistic and literary heritage. The loss was total.

There was a blessing in disguise, however. Thanks to English, a window on the world of knowledge opened. The Punjabis studying abroad in the universities of Oxford, Cambridge, London and California established contact and interaction with Western thought. In the early twentieth century Puran Singh (1881–1931), the poet, was writing on Nietzsche in Punjabi; Kahan Singh (1861–1938), the great lexicographer, was collaborating with Macauliffe (1837–1913), on the English translation of the Sikh scriptures for his six-volume magnum opus *The Sikh Religion*; Dharam Anant [Singh], the Greek and Sanskrit scholar, worked on Plato, and Santokh Singh (1892–1927) introduced Marx in Punjabi. Two collections of Puran Singh's poetry, and Dharam Anant's treatise on Plato and Sikhism were published in London by J.M. Dent and Luzac. Mulk Raj Anand moved in the Bloomsbury literary group. Khushwant Singh, Ved Mehta and Zulfikar Ghose made their mark on English literature in the latter half of the last century.

II

On this sundry background of gain and loss, I started writing at the age of twenty in my own language Punjabi, which I had learnt simultaneously with English. I cut my literary teeth in a real Punjabi milieu. My father, a carpenter turned photographer and communist trade unionist, wrote poetry as well. My mother was illiterate. So my home language remained unadulterated.

I rarely write poems in English. The ones I have written were for my loved ones who did not know my language. When I translate such poems into Punjabi, I put the appendage sheepishly – 'translated from English'. Of course Punjabi is my mother language. I think, feel and dream in it. I live in it and I will die in it. No wonder, working with English poets, I could translate only one fourth of my original poems into English. Kundera, in his novel *Testaments Betrayed*, sympathises and bemoans Leoš Janáček's determination to write his operas in Czech, thus limiting his audience. I feel that I am of his tribe.

The word for 'translation' in Punjabi is *anuvaad*. It is derived from Sanskrit *Anu*, meaning: which follows, close, near, corresponding, at the same time; and *vaad* is the idea behind a sound. The sound is the uttered word. The written word is silent. The poetic creative process can be defined in so many ways. Maybe the idea underlying the word *anuvaad* equally applies to the birth of a poem. Here an imagined reality takes shape in words.

Perhaps my most recent poem written in English could relate that experience.

To Father

As you taught me to write the first letter
    of Gurmukhi – the Punjabi script
holding my nervous hand in yours
You taught me to hold the camera
        to focus on faces   in the pupil of the eye
and to press the button   holding my breath

As if it were a gun
        loaded with bullets of life.

Where are you now, father?
Can you take some time off from death?

I'd like to take my self-portrait sitting next to you
    with a glint in my eyes.
Remember that photograph you took with the self-timer
    of us together many years ago
You holding me cheek to cheek?

The photograph doesn't show the lump in your throat.

We'll exchange pictures I have taken
  of faces you haven't seen
        and of places you never visited
and you can show me yours taken in the valley of the dead.

I was at the launch of the book of poems *The Eastern Boroughs* by John Welch at his place in Hackney. John introduced me to Libby Hall, a close friend of John Berger, saying that I was his greatest fan. I could not agree and said there must be many admirers like me. Unlike at other gatherings, I felt at ease and talked with Libby about John. She mentioned a recent unpublished essay of his about his father. I had never read any such essay on his father. Lost in my thoughts, I picked up some words uttered by Libby, like John whispering to the faded ink of his father's writing. It was too moving. I left early. On my way to Rectory Road Station the above poem was taking shape. I sat on the bench and started scribbling. While writing I was wondering why I was talking to my father in English? Maybe because Berger had inspired it; maybe because there were some words and images founded on my father's skills in photography that may have sounded bizarre in Punjabi. I was breaking bread with the dead, as Auden said about writing.

I sent the poem to Berger. He wrote back: 'I find your poem so beautiful – like an avenue in a city I was wanting to reach. Thank you for it. And tell your father I thank him.'

Reading these words from my mentor, I felt reassured that it had worked in English – the *akhand sphota* – undivided intuitive perception of the whole meaning – as postulated by Bhartrhari, the great Sanskrit linguist of 5th-6th century AD.

Itsik Manger
Four Poems
With three translations and one literal version

Introduced by Helen Beer

Itsik Manger (1901–1969) was one of the most gifted and popular Yiddish poets of the twentieth century. Despite the post-Holocaust depletion in the numbers of Yiddish speakers and readers, his writing has continued to be read, studied, performed and translated since his death. He also wrote prose, literary essays and drama, and created dialogue and lyrics for Yiddish films.

Manger's life mirrors the political and cultural upheaval which confronted his generation of East European Jews. Born in Czernowitz when it was part of the Austro-Hungarian Empire, he witnessed its becoming part of a Greater Romania in 1918. Like many Yiddish writers, Manger was drawn to Warsaw's flourishing Yiddish culture and he moved to Poland in 1928 where he remained for a decade. He spent two years in France from where he unsuccessfully tried to reach Palestine and the United States. He arrived in England in 1940 and remained there until 1951. Then followed a further ten years in the United States and several years in Israel prior to his death in 1969.

Many Yiddish writers made their first literary attempts in languages other than Yiddish: Manger's earliest poems, at the age of fifteen, were in German. He soon switched to Yiddish, his native tongue, and thereby began to inhabit a rich cultural world which transgressed any national or geographical boundaries. Despite the conscious choice to immerse himself in a Yiddish expression, Manger maintained links with other non-Yiddish writers and translated German and Romanian poets into Yiddish. His own poetry was translated into German (Alfred Magula-Sperber, Rosa Auslender) and other languages. For a long period he gathered folk songs of many cultures which he 're-composed' rather than translated.

Manger's years in Poland were his most productive; he wrote and published more there than in any subsequent period. Like many Yiddish writers at the time, he gave lectures and readings. In Poland, Manger felt he 'belonged' as a Yiddish poet to a dynamic Yiddish-speaking people.

Throughout his youth, Manger identified with the marginalised and the dispossessed. From the time of his departure to France and beyond, his life was one of displacement and exile. His sense of homelessness intensified and contributed to a particular psychological or existential condition, evident in his writing. Displacement and radical change, so frequently implicit in modern Yiddish writing, was often expressed as an identification with the past or as a rebellion against it. Manger's writing sought to find meaning at a particular moment in the history of a culture in which both the past and present combined.

Manger's particular skill as a poet lay in his ability to construct deceptively simple verse, often in a folk style. He drew material from Jewish and Yiddish religious and folk culture, often employing colloquial language and simple song metres. More than any other Yiddish poet, he concentrated on the ballad. By the twentieth century, the ballad may have seemed to be an archaic choice for a modern poet. Manger felt that Yiddish culture lacked this genre and he attempted to reverse this deficiency. He knew folk and literary ballads from many cultures and was conversant with world literature. His own penchant for storytelling and for the dramatic was compatible with ballad writing. Ballads, with their focus on a tragic event, were a suitable conduit for Manger's exploration of the tragic in life.

Manger's earlier ballads are more closely linked to traditional European folk ballads and to German literary ballads in particular. Many of his ballads adopt a traditional form; but he rapidly subverts it to serve his own ends. He often shifts between the impersonal narration of the traditional ballad and the more personal lyric voice of the modern poet. As conditions worsened for Jews in the 1930s, Manger consciously discarded 'foreign' influences in his writing in favour of retreating into a Jewish expression. After the outbreak of the Second World War, he rarely wrote ballads. He announced that as life itself was creating ballads, he was switching over to the sonnet.

The war in Europe and Manger's attempts to reach safety marked a turning point in his life and career. His arrival in London was marred by the homelessness he had endured since leaving Poland and by a struggle for survival. His partner in Poland, the writer and journalist Rachel Auerbach, had remained in Warsaw; he did not know the whereabouts of his father, brother and sister in Romania.

Manger became friends with Margaret Waterhouse (said to be the great-granddaughter of Mary and Percy Shelley) who ran an antiquarian bookshop in Swiss Cottage. She took him in and saw it as her mission to help the Yiddish poet. He communicated with her in English and seriously began to study English language and literature (already in Poland, he was able to recite Shakespeare in English). Manger read his poems in Yiddish to Margaret and to other non-Jewish friends and translated some into English ('Now I will sing for

Margaret / this sad little song / About a Jewish tailor-lad / who rang the evening bells / Ding-dong, Ding-dong . . .'). He planned an anthology of English poetry in Yiddish translation (from Herrick to Burns) which never materialised. The last volume of his poetry published in London in 1948 as a tribute to his brother Notte, now known to be dead, did not sell well. It was too difficult for most local Yiddish readers.

In London, Manger got to know Yiddish writers and enthusiasts, non-Jewish editors, writers and intellectuals. Arthur Waley began to study Yiddish with the aim of translating Manger's work into English (Manger's English was not yet good enough to do that himself). Isaac Deutscher thought that Manger should write a short book on Yiddish literature but could not get the backing. In 1950, at a meeting of the PEN club in Edinburgh, Manger became friends with Dan Davin, who later became Editor of Oxford University Press. They discussed ideas for an Oxford Book of Yiddish Verse, but could not get support for the project. But in 1987, at Davin's initiative, this became the *Penguin Book of Modern Yiddish Verse*.

Manger's poetry published in London reflects the constant movement he underwent during the war and after. It expresses sadness, regret, tragedy and outrage. There are poems and cycles of poems dedicated to all those he loved. During and immediately after the war, Manger was cautious in writing about the Holocaust, although when he did, it was with great impact. I have met several people who recall the following lines spoken by Manger, by way of an assessment of his life up until and including the London period:

'In Czernowitz geborn / in Varshe gevorn / in London farlorn'
('Born in Czernowitz / Became in Warsaw / Lost in London')

From the time that Manger achieved recognition as a Yiddish poet while still living in Romania, there was never any serious question that he should write in any language other than Yiddish. He had absorbed Yiddish language and culture from home and his reputation as a writer continued to grow during the unprecedented explosion of modern Yiddish culture in the inter-war period. For a generation of Jews who had distanced themselves from the traditional religious observance of their parents and grandparents, secular Yiddish culture was often seen as a way to cultural continuity, autonomy, unity and a broader secular learning; and as an antidote to war and oppression.

With the dramatic disappearance of Yiddish speakers after the war, Manger (and other Yiddish writers) had to reckon with depleted audiences and a limited readership. Poets responding to the tragic loss of millions of Yiddish speakers came to personify the language itself by describing Yiddish for example, as beautiful, homely, bereft and abandoned. In a sonnet titled 'Yiddish', Manger wrote:

Yidish, sheyne yoireshte fun undzer hoyz,
dayn sheynkeyt iz eynzam, dayn eynzamkeyt iz groys,
s'ara vunder vos dayn harts hot nokh nisht geplatst.
(Yiddish, beautiful heiress of our old house,
Your beauty is lonely, your loneliness is vast,
It is a wonder that your heart has not yet burst.)

For a brief period, when Manger's attempts to reach the USA were unsuccessful and he felt he was being obstructed by the American Yiddish writers, he threatened to sever all ties with Yiddish and never to write in the wretched 'jargon' again. When he finally arrived in America in 1951, he was well-received and his lectures and poetry readings were very well-attended. By his own admission, this was to be the most sterile period of his literary career; he wrote and published less than at any other previous time. In 1952 a selection of the poetry taken from all earlier collections was published in New York as one large volume, *Lid un balade*.

With his final move to Israel in the 1960s, Manger was accorded the recognition which he felt he had for so long been denied and which most closely resembled the reception he had enjoyed in Poland. By this time, he was too ill to actively renew his working life as a poet.

With his regular rhymes and rhythms, Manger can seem a neo-romantic poet, who wrote verse with clear links to folklore and popular culture. And yet he was modern, without being a modernist. Manger's is a lyrical voice, quietly and disturbingly indignant rather than revolutionary and dissonant. His persona, often at the centre of his poetry, speaks for the outcast and the rebel, but is linked to the past and not to the future.

di balade fun di toesn

kranker kop in nakhtishn fenster,
hent rufn got un oygn geshpenster.

shteyt oyfn dakh fun der nakhtisher shil
a shames, vos noygt zikh un ruft in der shtil

'in shul arayn vemen s'shrekt di nakht!
dos likhtl in kloyz, hob ikh oysgetrakht.'

kletert akegn oyf kloyster-vant
a galekh a shvartser, dem tsyelem in hant.

'in kloyster arayn vemen s'shrekt di nakht!
dos likhtl vos brent hob ikh oysgetrakht.'

fibert di nakht der vint un der regn
kumen tsu shvimen fun vegn un shtegn

a heyfele goyim a heyfele yidn
fun nakht aziln, fun merk un yaridn.

tapn zey blinde un zukhn di tirn –
'ver s'hot gerufn – der zol undz firn!'

blitst oyf a rege a toes-shayn –
geyen di goyim in shul arayn.

blitst oyf a rege a toes-shayn –
geyen di yidn in kloyster arayn.

fariglt di nakht hinter ale di tirn –
dos likht vos ken rufn, dos likht ken farfirn.

tseveynt zikh der kop in nakhtishn fenster,
kop vos trakht got un zet eybik geshpenster.

Ballad of the Errors

A sick head in the night window cries
For God in its prayers, for ghosts with its eyes.

There's a *shames* on the synagogue roof tonight,
He leans in the silence and he calls out

'Into the synagogue if you fear the night!
In the house of prayer I created the light.'

Up the church wall opposite clambers a priest,
A priest in black with a cross in his fist:

'Into the church if you fear the night!
I created its burning light.'

The night's in a fever, in the wind and the rain
There come together down street and lane

A handful of Gentiles, a handful of Jews
From fairs and markets, kips and stews,

They grope in the dark, they seek the door:
'He should guide us who called us here!'

Comes a sudden light, a phantom show,
Into the synagogue the Gentiles go.

Comes a sudden light, a phantom show,
Into the church the Jews go.

The night bolts the doors on one and all,
The light that beckons leads wrong as well.

The head in the window weeps. It sees
God in its thoughts but ghosts with its eyes.

Tsayt Balade

in mitn veg a kind a toyts
a meydele mit blonde hor.
nokh finef vokhn oder zeks –
volt es gevorn zibn yor.
der marshal gering shpilt zikh mit zayn kind.

di mame shteyt in mitn veg
un brekht die blaykhe dare hent,
zi hot gezen di shtot farvist,
zi hot gezen di heym farbrent.
der marshal gering shpilt zikh mit zayn kind.

un furlekh shlepn zikh farbay
mit hak un pak oyf na-venad,
vogler zenen ale di,
vos hobn ersht a heym gehat.
der marshal gering shpilt zikh mit zayn kind.

der poyer hot farlozt dos dorf,
der shtot-mentsh hot farlozt di shtot,
ver mit aks un ver tsu fus
vandert itst oyf gots barot.
der marshal gering shpilt zikh mit zayn kind.

die mame shteyt in mitn veg
neyn un neyn, zi vet nisht geyn.
vi lozt men dos in mitn veg
dos shlofndike kind aleyn?
der marshal gering shpilt zikh mit zayn kind.

zi zetst zikh nebn toytn kind
farviklt in ir groen shal.
di harbst-levone ibern vald –
a groyser zilberner medal.
der marshal gering shpilt zikh mit zayn kind.

der marshal zingt: 'mayn tekhterl,
dayn tate iz a blonder ber'
un far zayn fenster trot bay trot
marshirt dos broyne militer.
der marshal gering shpilt zikh mit zayn kind.

di mame zingt: 'mayn tekhterl,
mayn gold, mayn kroyn un mayn farmeg,
dayn mame iz a verbe itst
vos troyert do in mitn veg.'
der marshal gering shpilt zikh mit zayn kind.

un vi a verbe roysht zi shtil
in troyer ibern toytn kind,
mit ire shvarts tselozte hor
shpilt zikh der september-vint.
der marshal gering shpilt zikh mit zayn kind.
der marshal zingt: 'mayn tekhterl,

dayn tate iz a feld-marshal'
di harbst-levone oyf zayn brust
blitst – a zilberner medal.
der marshal gering sphilt zikh mit zayn kind.

di mame zingt: 'mayn tekhterl,
mayn kind, mayn fri farloshn kind,
dayn mame iz a sove itst
vos klogt ir veytik farn vint.'
der marshal gering shpilt zikh mit zayn kind.

* * *

dos dozike lid hob ikh fartrakht
in london in a hospital,
dos lid fun toytn kind in veg
un fun dem fetn feld-marshal,
vos toyt, un shpilt zikh mit zayn kind.

Ballad of the Times

There's a dead child lying in the road,
A little girl with blond hair.
Five or six weeks more maybe
She'd have reached her seventh year.
Marshal Goering is playing with his child.

The mother is standing in the road,
She wrings her white hands thin with grief.
She saw the town unpeopled
And flames come through her roof.
Marshal Goering is playing with his child.

And carts and wagons are dragging past
With bags and baggage and they must go
Wandering the roads who had
A house and home an hour ago.
Marshal Goering is playing with his child.

The village has and the town has
Lost all the people who lived there
Who now must ride or walk to know
What mercy God can spare.
Marshal Goering is playing with his child.

The mother is standing in the road
And there she will remain
For who'd leave lying in the road
Her sleeping child alone?
Marshal Goering is playing with his child.

She sits, she wraps her dead child round
In her grey shawl until
Above the wood there's an autumn moon
Like a big and silver medal.
Marshal Goering is playing with his child.

The Marshal sings: Little girl of mine
Your father is a blond bear.
Under his window the brown army
Tramp-tramp away to war.
Marshal Goering is playing with his child.

The mother sings: Little girl of mine
My gold, my crown, my everything
Your mother is a willow tree
By the roadside weeping.
Marshal Goering is playing with his child.

And over her dead child she bows
Grieving like a willow there
And the breezes of September play
With her black unfastened hair.
Marshal Goering is playing with his child.

The Marshal sings: Little girl of mine
Your father is a field marshal,
The harvest moon that shines upon
His breast is a silver medal.
Marshal Goering is playing with his child.

The mother sings: Little girl of mine
My child, my daughter dead so soon
Your mother is an owl now
And tells the wind her pain.
Marshal Goering is playing with his child.

* * *

This is a song that I thought up
In London, in a hospital,
The song of the dead child in the road
And the fat field marshal
Who kills, and plays with his child.

London, 1940

Auld Lang Syne

mir zingen ineynem 'auld lang syne'
un mir haltn zikh bay di hent.
der vayn in di glezer finklt royt,
dos likht in di shpiglen blendt.

ikh zing oyf a kol 'for auld lang syne'
mit oygn farveynte, royte –
ikh zing mit aykh, un halt bay di hent
mayne milyonen toyte.

Auld Lang Syne

We take one another by the hand
And sing an 'Auld Lang Syne'.
The mirror blinds the eyes with lights,
They sparkle in our red wine.

'For Auld Lang Syne', I sing it loud
Weeping, my eyes are red.
I sing with you and hold your hands
My millions of dead.

tsinishe idilye

dray turistn bay di khurves fun geto,
vu s'hot gehulyet der daytscher mord,
an eltere mis, a nyu yorker bankir,
un an alter englisher lord.

di eltere mis veynt arayn in ir tikhl,
a kalte trer farvyanet un gel,
in ir hant-tash an englisher baybl
'got' un 'pipl of israel'.

meri . . . di heylike yidishe mame,
dzizus . . . dos heylike yidishe kind.
pontus pilatus, der roymisher mamzer,
vos sreyfet in gehenem far zayne zind.

der nyu-yorker bankir nemt arop fotos
fun di farblutikte geto-vent,
in moyl – tsvey shures goldene tseyn
un goldene ringen oyf di hent.

di fotos nemt er far zayn bas yekhide,
vos endikt hay-skul iber a yor.
zayn tokhter doris iz shlank vi a tseder,
un hot roytlekhe titsian-hor.

der alter lord shvaygt vi a mumye,
a rendl mit zibetsn shiling a vort,
er trakht fun zayn mayontek in stratford,
un nakhest di tsikhtik-farkemte bord.

er trakht fun zayn zun dem takhshit in oksford,
vos vet nokh mistome mit der tsayt
haltn a 'spitsh' in hoyz of lords,
a sheyndl far britishe odl-layt.

der ovnt tunklt. in di khurves fun geto
nestn zikh soves un fleder-mayz fleen,
di dray turistn nemen dem ekspres tsug,
un forn farbrengen in freylekhn berlin.

Cynical Idyll

Three tourists in the ruins of the ghetto
Where German murder revelled,
An elderly miss, a New York banker
And an old English lord.

The elderly miss cries into her hankie
A cold tear faded and yellow,
In her handbag an English bible
'God' and 'People of Israel'.

Mary ... the holy Jewish mother,
Jesus ... the holy Jewish child.
Pontius Pilate, the Roman bastard,
Who burns in hell for his sins.

The New York banker takes photos
Of the bloodied ghetto walls,
In his mouth – two rows of golden teeth
And golden rings on his hands.

The photos he takes for his only daughter,
Who'll finish high school next year
His daughter Doris is tall as a cedar
And has reddish Titian-hair.

The old lord is silent as a mummy,
A ducat and seven shillings a word,
He is thinking of his fortune in Stratford
And takes pride in his chic groomed beard.

He thinks of his son, his jewel, in Oxford
Who will most likely in time
Give a speech in the House of Lords
An ornament of British nobility.

The evening darkens. In the ruins of the ghetto
Owls nest and bats are flying.
The three tourists take the express train
And go for amusement to jolly Berlin.

Michael Hamburger
Afterthoughts on the Mug's Game

To me, my life and work are a jigsaw puzzle with more pieces than I can ever put together. I tried once, some thirty years ago now, for a book about my early years I called not an autobiography but 'intermittent memoirs' – intermittent because even then I was too conscious of the holes in my memory that could not be filled with the documentary evidence I did my best to collect. One reason why I never wrote the projected sequel about later years is that my own case became less and less interesting to me, except as a gauge of phenomena and developments outside myself that did continue to concern me. But the essence of such experience had gone into my chosen medium of verse, by that process of condensation which Ezra Pound distinguished from the process of functional prose by deriving the German word 'dichten' – to make poetry – from the adjective 'dicht' – dense or tight. This etymology is spurious, but 'ben trovato'. Pound's enemies could have pointed out that 'dichten' derived from nothing less prosaic than 'dictare', probably going on to connect this derivation with Pound's leaning towards dictators. Even thirty years ago I also knew that any autobiography I could have written would have been a work of fiction – a selection from the events and concerns of my life and work, a collaboration of memory with imagination, with which it is inextricably bound up; not a chronicle, like the one I had attempted, but a transmutation of the material. And after one abortive novel written in my youth I recognised once and for all that a full-length work of prose fiction was not for me – not even as a translator!

By 1972 I had also begun my retreat from the literary scene in Britain and the USA, with the consequence that my book of memoirs received no more attention than my books of poems in Britain, and none at all in the USA, where the book was not published, and that my British publisher at the time was discouraging about the sequel or complement I might have produced. Then, in my later middle age, after the Thatcherite cultural revolution, I did experience something like alienation, feeling that all I had done or might still do had no place or function in the new order. Over the centuries, the British institutions had been formed by a tug between conservative pieties – dismissed as hypocritical or snobbish by those who did not share them – and radical ferment, leading to compromises and equipoises like the capacious Anglican Church with its many mansions, a monarchy hedged in not by a constitution but by parliamentary proceedings, and our post-war welfare state, in which class differences were levelled upwards, generously and benevolently. The new money free-for-all put an end to both traditions. Old conservatives who had assented to the welfare state, together with Liberals and Socialists, were eliminated one by one as 'wets'. 'Democratic' was confused with 'demotic', the culture levelled down, 'dumbed down'. The new 'Conservatism' was as little about the conservation of anything but the growth of profits as New Labour was to be about productive skills and labour or the radical tradition it found it expedient to incorporate into its name. 'Modernization' now meant not progress in any direction – the culture itself having become 'post-modern' – but the maximization of profits. In this would-be egalitarian society a new under-class was created, that of the losers in the rat race, now excluded from the solidarity that had sustained the former working classes, who since the nineteenth century had become upwardly mobile by education, self-education fostered by their social 'superiors'.

Anything I could now write in plain prose – or plain verse, for that matter – had become too plain to be noticed or understood, when double-talk, duplicity, 'spin', 'sound-bites', and 'rip-off' had taken over in the public realm; and for most of those at the receiving end – always and everywhere – it's less uncomfortable to make what use they can of a devalued coinage than to reject and resist it. In that climate it was best for me to concentrate on the 'non-events' of my latest long poem, cultivating that silence from which the music of poetry has always sprung, with only rare intrusions of other noises.

Here I can't help thinking of my paternal grandfather, who had written under the family name or the pseudonym Burghammer. My mother told me that before he died, at about the time of my birth, he had not only been silenced as a writer by the pressures of earning a living, but reduced to total silence by the professional dishonour inflicted on him by two of his five children, a dishonour that broke his heart. If, more than once, my heart came close to being broken, it was also mended again and again, by love and defiance. Had my grandfather been a poet, rather than a critic and a mediator, even his terminal silence could have elicited words of a kind – words addressed to no one or anyone.

So I doubt that my case would have been essentially different if I had not been displaced at the age of nine from one country, one language, to another. I can imagine no personal or literary development in the world as it is that could run in a straight line or a closed circle. When I still practised literary criticism, which I have given up, I looked for the truth about writers in their contradictions, that quarrel with oneself which Yeats said generates poetry, as distinct from rhetoric – though Yeats may now seem a rhetorical poet. My one book-length critical work, *The Truth of Poetry* was a study in tensions and extremes that clashed and met either within the work of a single writer or in the possibilities of all poetry within the temporal and linguistic bounds of my enquiry. In order to write that book, over a period of at least ten years, I had to break with my academic specialisation as a teacher of German, in which I had always felt uncomfortable – as in any specialisation whatever, other than in the craft of poetry, the mug's game to which I had chosen to devote my life.

A Mug's Game was the title of my book of memoirs, the first version of it, though I changed the title for a second version published in 1991, not wishing by then to make too much of its derivation from a remark by T.S. Eliot about the vocation, and substituting a title drawn from a poem of mine, *String of Beginnings*. Though the Eliot epigraph, too, had to be replaced, all my later experience had confirmed its truth – not only for Eliot but for poets less eminent than he was when he made a remark so uncharacteristically personal and confessional, however general its formulations: 'As things are, and as fundamentally they must always be, poetry is not a career but a mug's game. No honest poet can ever feel quite sure of the permanent value of what he has written: he may have wasted his time and messed up his life for nothing.'

Well, not only did the posthumous edition of Eliot's letters have to be suspended after one volume, because it had come up against a consensus adverse to him, but 'permanent value' had become too big a mouthful for any poet to perpetrate in public, even if in his or her heart it remains the only possible incentive and justification for what cannot be a career. At the height of his fame T.S. Eliot had been invited to address the Conservative Party, on the strength of his professed allegiance to the established Church and the monarchy. It was to be a government that called itself Conservative which made the royal family subject to income tax, therefore competitive in the market economy and symbolically redundant. T.S. Eliot will have turned in his grave.

The aspiration to the (immortal) fame which to Milton was

'that last infirmity of noble mind' became mere delusion and vanity when fame had turned into instant, promiscuous and often fortuitous celebrity; and even before that state of affairs it had been quite possible for a poet to keep up the mug's game in total obscurity or rejection. At the age of eighteen or nineteen in a Soho pub, I asked my friend John Heath-Stubbs whether he had ever had a poem anthologized, thinking in my naivety that this made all the difference between being called and being chosen. A few decades later I had to clear out a hundred contributor's copies of anthologies in which I was represented with poems or translations, keeping only those I thought of some significance. Decades after that, far from having graduated to immortality by anthologization, I had amassed a new lumber of such volumes, including many in foreign languages or scripts in which I can't even make out my name – from Arabic to Chinese; but in my country was now omitted as a poet from all anthologies treated as representative. Cultural correctness now disposed of me with the phrase 'better known as a translator' or simply ignored the poems I have written. The same cultural correctness now tends to be racist, nationalistic, sexist (or genderist, to use the current term), classist and agist, perpetually rubbing in the differences while proclaiming a would-be egalitarianism. (Real equality begins where it's taken for granted, not asserted or enforced.) Whatever competent or distinguished critics had written about my work in the past, these omissions could always be justified on other grounds, the dubious 'permanent value' a poet can never be sure about in his or her own case; and criticism itself has been largely diverted from texts to the personalities of their authors.

The most dramatic change since T.S. Eliot's lifetime is the degree to which electronic media have replaced the written word – and the spoken word, for that matter, where it has become a gabble in competition with the abbreviations of those media, because time is money. The effect of this on generations that receive most of their knowledge not from immediate experience, nor from original texts, but from the television screen or from computers is so blatant that it needs no elaboration here. Its effect on poetry – its reception, if not its production – is not only a psychic one, in that more and more young people have grown incapable of sustained attention to anything whatever, other than images and sounds projected for instant consumption or instant distraction – distraction from what, one begins to ask oneself – but a practical one that extends to the non-career. The internet is not subject to those copyright laws that gave authors some measure of control over the use of their work and a minimal share in the form of royalties or fees. If a poem is used on a website the author need not be so much as informed, let alone paid for a publication now treated as an advertisement; and even the most vain of authors cannot live by advertisement alone. Needless to add, the question of 'permanent value' does not arise at all in media that are random, insatiably and indigestibly cumulative, conveying information about this, that and anything without end.

I have written elsewhere – in an essay included in my book *Testimonies* of 1988 – about the survival of poetry in historical circumstances or conditions of which I am aware. Poems were written or recited even in extermination camps – or preserved in one person's memory, like the later poems of Mandelstam. As long ago as the first industrial revolution in Britain, the end of poetry was predicted, as by Thomas Carlyle. The prediction was proved wrong, both because the squalor brought in by that revolution created a need to escape from it – the Romantic movement – and because an expanding readership, even for poetry, could be served by the mass production of written texts. The reversal of that development may now look like the end of a whole culture, the literate one, in which literacy was bound up with an awareness of the past – a selected past, therefore 'elitist' in the terminology of those who confuse class resentments with considerations of quality. This reversal is still resisted here and there, by dwindling minorities; but other threats of environmental, economic and political disasters detract again and again from the urgency of the resistance, not that it is not the continuity of one culture, one civilization, but of life on our planet that is in question. Any prediction about the future of poetry would rest on the complacent assumption that the larger destruction can still be averted.

So much had to be said before I could bring myself to write anything more about my own case, displacement from Germany to Britain in childhood, or the multilingualism that seems as natural to me as the opposite seems to others. Throughout a millennium and more, educated Europeans had to be proficient in a dead language, Latin, if not Greek and Hebrew also – a Latin which was not dead where it functioned as the *lingua franca* in the Babel of modern languages and dialects in Europe and beyond – much as English can still do in India. Milton wrote poems in Italian, and in the next century William Cowper translated Milton's Italian and Latin poems into English, the language in which both of them had been born to speak and write.

What's more, migration, dispersal and resettlement have become the rule, rather than the exception, in many parts of the world, as throughout recorded history, not least that of Britain and American. When a Welsh nationalist critic described me as a 'rootless cosmopolitan', I had to tell him that in fact I had become a stick-in-the-mud as a poet, drawing most of my imagery from a single region of England that has become my home. It is plants, not human beings, that are physically rooted; and long ago Remy de Gourmont distinguished the uprooted – déracinés – from the transplanted. This applies even to non-human nature, plants and animals. Most of the trees most wide-spread in Britain were introduced from foreign parts at one time or another. One of the most prolific weeds or wildflowers in Britain and continental Europe now is the Himalayan balsam. An American grey squirrel has displaced the European red squirrel in all but the wildest parts of Britain. One of our commonest birds now is the collared dove which until a few decades ago was confined to Eastern

Europe. Until exterminated by genocide, the South American coypu, a large vegetarian rodent, spread all over the East Anglian marshlands on which I live. In my East Anglian garden, exposed to fierce winds from the North Sea, trees from America, even Mexico and Nicaragua, as from China and Japan, do as well as trees regarded as indigenous since the records began. Much the same is true of culture and the arts, from agriculture and horticulture, their products and implements, to architecture, sculpture, painting, musical composition and the verse forms dear to traditionalists.

As for me, my bibliography attests that I have translated and written about more German language authors than I can enumerate here. Though at school I began to specialize in Modern Languages, I could not take up the Exhibition (scholarship) I had won to Christ Church, Oxford, without passing an entrance examination in what is not a modern language, Latin, still obligatory at that time, 1941, for students of any subject, and in retrospect I wish that my early specialization had not been forced on me, at the expense of the Ancient Greek I should otherwise have learnt. The first and main modern language I did learn was French, and there was a time when my French was better than what remained of my childhood German and the book German that complemented it. My first book of translations, completed at the age of eighteen and published when I was nineteen, was from the German poet Hölderlin, on whose difficult texts I was to go on working off and on for half a century; but my second book of translations was from the French of Baudelaire, done in 1944 when I was an infantry soldier in the Shetlands, and still in print with an American publisher, City Lights. With very few exceptions, foreign influences on my earliest poems were more French than German. What impelled me to make German my main subject when I returned to Oxford after military service was my renewed contact with the spoken language as an interpreter for German prisoners-of-war in Austria and as headmaster of an Army boarding school staffed with Austrian civilians, as well as British teachers. As a soldier in Italy I had also taken up Italian, at first by reading Dante in a bilingual text that could easily be carried in a kitbag, the Temple Classics edition. Though it was already too late for me to pick up another language in the way I had plunged into English as a boy, I was to translate one Italian poet, Franco Fortini, with his help and the odd howler, a few Italian poems by others needed for my critical book and – more recently – two poems by Leopardi I had long lived with. More recently still it was some lines of Dante used as an epigraph for the latest book I have translated, W.G. Sebald's *After Nature*, which also called for a version of a Latin epigraph from Vergil. *The Truth of Poetry* has also elicited versions of poems in Spanish and Portuguese, languages I can't begin to speak. When the Romanian poet Marin Sorescu asked me to translate poems of his, I was able to do so because Romanian is a partly Romance language and because the virtuoso German poet Oskar Pastior allowed me to cannibalize his excellent German versions of these poems. When I tried to translate from languages I can neither speak nor guess at, by way of literal cribs or trots, I found myself groping in the dark for Hungarian and liberated by ignorance for the one poem I was asked to translate from the Chinese, so much so that I could place this version in my *Collected Poems* and it has been translated in turn into German as a poem of my own – a *chinoiserie*. Because my curiosity about the state of post-war Europe drove me into Displaced Persons' Camps out of bounds to British soldiers in Austria, camps filled with refugees from the Baltic, Ukraine and Tito's Yugoslavia, I was brought up against the limits of my capacity to absorb more languages, including Russian. It had been hard enough at first to adjust to the Carinthian dialect, when my brain sponge was reaching saturation point for languages.

Here I must mention that when I was presented with a gold medal by the Society of Linguists, only its receipt by post saved me from having to refuse it or suffering painful embarrassment at its presentation, since I don't think of myself as a linguist at all, only as person with a boundless interest in what can be communicated and not communicated verbally, in literary texts or other media. From earliest childhood onwards this interest extended to animals and mute plants. In later years I wrote a poem called 'Conversation with a Blackbird', only one of several in which I tried to transcribe or translate animal sounds. So the many translations I have done, to me, were not linguistic exercises but responses to the most diverse phenomena – explorations less of affinities than of strangeness. The more difficult and strange a text, the more challenging it was likely to prove, like the texts of Hölderlin and Celan. From Celan's poems I could take nothing I am aware of for my own; from Hölderlin nothing more palpable than a way of breathing. Accessibility, in that process, had more to do with empathy than with knowledge of any kind, linguistic, historical or textual.

The crux of my displacement at the age of nine, from Berlin to Edinburgh, is that it occurred at an age when adjustment is either immediate or impossible. I compared the sudden change to a child's being thrown into water so that it can learn to swim – for survival. My Berlin childhood had been so oppressed by restrictions, even before the Third Reich, that when I was quite able to swim I dropped like a stone into the water of the Havel, at Kladow outside Berlin, and had to be rescued from an unconscious wish to drown by the second of the governesses who had oppressed us – not a benevolent disciplinarian like our first, but a sadistic one with a resentment that had contributed to my state of mind. In Edinburgh, without a governess at last, I recovered my will to survive. This meant acceptance into a community of schoolboys, made possible only by almost immediate linguistic assimilation – and by my plunge from the highest springboard of a swimming-pool, to the admiration of my fellow pupils not as familiar as I was with water, thanks to my grandfather's house at Kladow and perhaps to earlier sea-side holidays on the Baltic coast. I was then invited to join a street gang from the school,

George Watson's, that picked fights with boys wearing the uniforms of other Edinburgh schools – when in Berlin my three siblings and I had never been allowed to go anywhere but to school without adult supervision, or play with children not approved by the supervisors.

So the fall from upper-middle-class prosperity and status – my father had been a professor of paediatrics as well as a family doctor, and in Germany professorships were prestigious – proved my liberation from an increasing introversion that had become morbid. But my father had to sit all day long over textbooks in a language still foreign to him during the year's crash course in all branches of medicine he had to absolve so as to be allowed to practise in Britain – where paediatricians did not work as family doctors and no professorship awaited him – on money borrowed to pay the rent of the furnished Edinburgh house, since he had made over what savings he had to his widowed mother, who stayed behind in Berlin until transported to her death, probably in Poland. All we ever knew, from a Red Cross message, was that she had 'gone on a journey'. Within a year of that, in 1940, my father succumbed to an incurable illness. Meanwhile, in a Britain still civil, I had been able to outgrow the necessary macho phase, though a few fights were still needed at later schools.

But the phases are recorded in my memoirs; also, that assimilation had governed my forebears ever since the eighteenth-century Enlightenment, the emancipation of the Jews from their ghettos and the Code Napoléon, whose solution to the 'Jewish Problem' was the opposite of Hitler's in that the Jews were to disappear not by genocide but by their absorption into the majority. This earlier trend was to be reversed, on the basis of a eugenics drawn from cattle-breeding, adopted out of resentment with mass appeal. Just because the ideology was absurd, it had to be implemented with an unprecedented thoroughness and bureaucratic efficiency, so that the method would justify the madness. Had the Third Reich lasted longer, its 'final solution' would have extended to those of partly 'non-Aryan' provenance, as intended, then those of Slavic or other non-Germanic descent. If it had, the German population itself would have been reduced not only to the 'purity' but to the size of an aboriginal tribe – a logical conclusion hardly compatible with world domination, quite apart from the losses incurred by war and the increasing risk of internal revolt.

What had not struck me when I wrote the memoirs was the French sympathies of both my grandfathers – one born in Prussian Silesia, the other in Mainz, in whose ghetto his ancestors had lived. My paternal grandfather, Leopold, attempted to introduce French Naturalism into Germany, a decade or more before there was a Naturalist movement in Germany, and long before the Dreyfus affair. Because all this grandfather's papers were lost when his widow was taken out of her Berlin flat, all I have of his literary remains is a few letters to him by Alphonse Daudet and Zola. (It was the editor of a book of Zola's letters who passed on what little he could discover about my grandfather's publications.) It can't have been an accident that my maternal grandfather's first name was Bertrand, and his father's Louis – both not German, but French forms; or that his grandfather, too, was a reader of Zola and other French writers.

The social assimilation, though, was such that I never saw the inside of a synagogue until my friend Erich von Kahler took me into one in New Jersey in the 1960s or 70s, not for worship but for a lay speech he was delivering there. When my paternal grandmother, born in Poland, spoke of going to the 'Temple', I imagined a Greek one. No one else in the family ever mentioned such a place. The very first prayer I learnt by heart was a childish jingle taught me by our Roman Catholic governess; and Hebrew was not among the languages of which I was given so much as a smattering. One of my great-uncles, who survived the Third Reich in Berlin, had become a Lutheran and married an 'Aryan' of the landowning class – killed there in a mugging after the war throughout which she had stuck by her 'non-Aryan' husband. Another great-uncle fled Berlin only at the last moment, surviving the war with his wife under an assumed name, with no ration cards, as itinerant farm labourers. That survival made a mockery of the biological race laws; assimilation had gone so far as to invalidate them in practice; and on a visit to my family after the war this great-uncle was outraged by an anti-German remark, leaping up from the dinner table to protest that he was still a German – after being condemned to death as such, robbed of his house and possessions, deprived even of the pointer hounds of whose loss he told us with tears not shed for his murdered human friends. My mother became a Quaker; and one of the last books read by my agnostic father was a selection of the works of Kierkegaard, when he was working on a psychological book he did not live to finish. (I was to write a little piece on Kierkegaard, included in my collection *Testimonies*.)

So it came about, too, that I was sent to distinctly Anglican schools after Edinburgh and spent most of my formative years in very British institutions – a Hampstead prep. school, a public school, Westminster – attached to the Abbey – Christ Church, Oxford – attached to the Cathedral – and the British Army – up to the age of twenty-four. As the poet I was already trying to become, I got some encouragement and assurance from being at a school, Westminster, which had produced poets for centuries, from Ben Jonson – a working-class pupil when the school was a truly public one – George Herbert, Henry King, among other excellent minor poets of the 'metaphysical' kind, to Dryden and Cowper, in the earlier centuries. It was a clever and precocious fellow pupil, Richard Wollheim, who read some of my first, and still somewhat Tennysonian, apprentice pieces and advised me to toughen up my verse by reading Dryden. My first published essay, written in 1942 or 1943, while I was waiting in London for my military call-up, was on 'John Donne and Metaphysical Poetry'; and my last academic job, in Britain, was a temporary part-time professorship that demanded only one weekly lecture and seminar on twentieth-century English and American poets.

My inflated early poems, which made up in rhetoric for what they lacked in sensuous roughage, also remind me how much, at this period, I took to heart the religious worship in which I participated in all those institutions, although I never became a member of any church or sect, and the theological teaching at Westminster, called 'Divinity', was decidedly liberal, if not positively ecumenical. Many later quarrels with myself were to arise between the life-long effects of this taking to heart and a need just as strong for independence of mind. The security to be found in any corporative membership had become suspect to me at an early age. If that was to leave me an outsider everywhere, in spite of loyalties that could not be formalised or formulated, so it had to be.

Because George Watson's had prided itself on 'pure', standard English, this was the vernacular into which I was initiated, and nothing was ever to shake that foundation, not even when my English had to become basic in the barrack-rooms I shared with other infantry privates, the lowest of the low in the class order only beginning to be loosened at that time. If my father's crash course had taken him to Glasgow, and my first British school had not been a private one, my linguistic initiation would have been very different indeed and my case complicated by regional, as well as class, divisions. Later, I was to teach some ten semesters at universities and colleges in the USA as a visiting professor, also travelling widely there for readings and lectures from New Hampshire to Texas, from Montana to South Carolina. Even in Britain this vernacular of mine had become an anachronism; but other vernaculars could serve me only for satirical or polemical purposes, the 'low mimetic' also demanded for solidarity in barrack-rooms – a small price to be paid for the considerateness and kindness I received in these, so that at times I could even work at poems while sitting or lying on a palliasse, no table or chair provided for the lowest of the low. However assimilated,

I never anglicized my surname, and didn't need to for these barrack-rooms; nor later, when my surname had become the name of a junk food, or because I was serving in a war against the country that gave my family that name.

My first translations may have been my way of bridging the displacement from that country, separation from the relatives and friends left behind, from the open spaces around Kladow to which I owed my first moments of freedom and exhilaration, the diverse animals I had collected and looked after there, and what had been my family's culture – though it was music, not language, that was my earliest love in the arts, and one practised by my father and mother. Had I been a few years older when the displacement occurred, I might well have had to return to my first language as a writer of poems. My friend Franz Wurm, born in Prague into a German-speaking family also fluent in Czech, was shipped to England in a children's transport at the age of thirteen and educated at an English boarding-school, then Oxford. Because, unlike me, he had lost his immediate family, when told by an English friend that he would never make a good English poet, he reverted not to German but to French for his early verse – his German lost to him by association with the more grievous loss. 'It was only then that I turned to German, which for quite a while came from my reading rather than from the language spoken at home,' he writes in a letter. He was then moved to re-emigrate to a German-speaking part of Switzerland, a neutral country by association, and became a German-language poet as linguistically inventive and idiosyncratic as his friend Paul Celan – who was even more multilingual by circumstance, but clung to German for poetry when he talked and corresponded with his wife and son in French, out of his very obsession with his *mother* tongue and the wound inflicted on his family and friends under German occupation. Erich Fried, one of the most widely read German-language poets of his time, came to England at the age of sixteen, remained resident there, but never became wholly bilingual other than as a translator of texts ranging from Shakespeare to Dylan Thomas and Sylvia Plath. Many other cases could be cited, each distinct for reasons too intricate to be unravelled here.

When towards the age of thirty, I was induced to write unambitious critical pieces in German, they proved acceptable, though my syntax, like my attitudes, tended to be more English than German and my grammar could be shaky; but the attempt to function bilingually, at least in prose, precipitated an identity crisis for a year or two, leaving me stranded in a no man's land. For a time I was able to produce German versions of English poems of mine that had found no other translator, or to collaborate with my earliest German translators if necessary. To resolve the crisis, though, I had to put an end to the pretence of bilingualism. The three tiny poems I wrote in German – for friends with little English – only brought home to me that my childish-cum-bookish German lacked the resources needed for poetry – resources of lived experience and association more than linguistic proficiency. For better or for worse, it is the English language in which I feel at home – its wealth of short words, its range of many-layered meanings, its laxities and lazinesses even, its shedding long ago of cases, declensions and inflections, its freedom from grammatical compulsions, leaving most English speakers scarcely aware that there is or was such as thing as grammatical rules, if they were never drilled in a foreign language as law-abiding as Latin or German. (Christian Morgenstern made fun of the bureaucratic and pedantic proclivities of his language in his well-known 'Werewolf' poem. The dadaist Kurt Schwitters subverted them in his best-known poem 'Anna Blume'.)

I, too, was told early on by a friend that no one not born in an English-speaking country would ever write a good English poem. I defied that warning as one of many risks incurred and defied throughout my life, not only by my choice of the mug's game. At a reading in Washington D.C. my fellow British poet George Macbeth introduced me as 'the best German poet writing in English', and I can never know whether that was a back-handed compliment of a kind I have got used to or a critical judgement. I also gathered from a recent four-volume German anthology of British and American poetry that I am the most widely translated poet – into German – of its living contributors. This, again, could be due to non-literary judgements, accidents of politico-cultural correctness or a generous act of restitution towards my person, and it could mean that the translatable gist of my poems does appeal more to German-language readers than to the English-speaking. Interesting as the sociology and psychology of reputations may be in themselves, after sixty years of the mug's game I can't speculate how they apply to my case. Whatever the reasons and motivations, I have received more prizes and more serious attention for my work in the German-speaking countries than in Britain; but this points to general differences in the status of the arts and the status of their practitioners. Poetry especially is an overcrowded occupation, because, as Keats wrote, there will always be too many of us, and it's simply too easy to produce something that looks like a poem but fails to sound or work like one. No wonder, then, that in Britain most of one's fellow practitioners – called 'colleagues' in Germany – turn out to be competitors, often mean ones at that. With his tongue in his cheek or not, the magnanimous English poet Geoffrey Hill once spoke of 'the rabble of one's so-called peers'. The book in which he did so, I was told, received no review in our country other than one I wrote. From Germany I receive letters in which the formal address 'geehrter' (honoured) is heightened to 'verehrter' (admired or revered). The British response to that is likely to be embarrassment or amusement, but there is more to it than an archaic formality. Because I cannot bring myself to enter for any of our countless poetry competitions, the prizes I have been awarded were unsolicited, therefore honours as well as subsidies. At a session of the Royal Society of Literature founded by a Hanoverian king to subsidize writers like Coleridge, who discovered very soon and painfully that the funds were no longer available, so that later elected Fellows of the society have had to pay a subscription fee for the honour – Lord Butler, its President at the time, presented a prize to John Wain for a book on Samuel Johnson, going on to say he was sorry to have gathered that John Wain now intended not to write another book of that kind but to return to his hobby of writing poems. Most German poets I have known would have felt this to be a disparagement of their chosen vocation. In England, for England, it was an instance of good sense – not a literary judgement or a personal one, but a confirmation, by a statesman, that the mug's game is not a career, since no living can be made by it.

In Britain this state of affairs makes for a humility that may or may not be a genuine one. There is a kind of pride, also known as integrity, that one must allow others to see as arrogance, just as there is a seeming humility, often combined with bonhomie and charm, that lends itself to opportunist climbing. No one could have been more proud in his dealings with the world than the poet of love and religious orthodoxy, Dante – humble enough, too, towards his pagan predecessor Vergil to make him his poetic guide – up to the point of separation.

This brings me to the mediating of mainly, but not exclusively German texts as a translator and critic – for which I was 'better known', at least until given later coverage in a British newspaper as a grower of mainly obsolete apple varieties. A few of the translations have been reprinted, enlarged and revised over a period that seems long for such work. Of my critical books only *The Truth of Poetry* remains in print in Britain, not in the USA, has appeared in German three times, Italian, Spanish in Mexico, and is about to appear in Portuguese in Brazil. In retrospect I wonder how I could possibly have turned out so many books – by choice, not commission – much of the time while doing odd jobs or teaching for a living, travelling not for relaxation but more work, with energy to spare for physical labour in gardens when we had gardens to tend, as we did most of the time. For the last twenty-four years it has been three and a half acres of land, on which I have planted more trees than I have published books; and I think it is the physical labour of their conservation that has kept me going to the age of eighty-one. Most translation and criticism are as ephemeral in effect as my cyclically repetitive gardening chores – and as one can't stop hoping a few of one's poems are not, with the potentiality at least of outlasting the grower like a tree.

Beyond that I have little to say about my translations and criticism, subject as both are to market forces, the reputation stock exchange, its brokers and the fluctuations of all these. Since auto-psychoanalysis is another mug's game that does not attract me, I shall not pretend to understand why or how I was drawn to one text rather than another. It is German-language critics who have tried to put the jigsaw puzzle pieces together in books and essays on my work – though a student of James Dickey in South Carolina came as close as anyone, for my early poems only, in the USA, telling me things I did not know about them. Every translation I have done and every critical piece I have written also belongs to the jigsaw puzzle, each a requirement of its own in the first place. If I can risk a generalization now, only about my translations from the German, it is that they were of texts I considered different in one way or another from anything written in English, therefore not unnecessary as additions to a literature already inexhaustible in its variety and range. It could be the few mediaeval lyrics I attempted by Walther von der Vogelweide, a baroque sonnet by Andreas Gryphius in lines so irregular that it does not look like a sonnet, or later poets to whom I devoted whole books; and it could be short prose by Novalis, Kleist, Büchner, Georg Heym or my contemporaries Eich, Grass, Heissenbüttel, Bichsel and Adolf Muschg unlike any others I know. Of my Goethe translations, plays and poems, the one that gave me most trouble and pleasure was the least-known, the late dramatic fragment *Pandora* in which each speech is in a metre appropriate to the mythical speaker, an invention that transcends the stage it was written for and in which the heroine never appears, though she is present throughout in the speakers' minds. Hofmannsthal's play *The Tower* is another play that strains the possibilities of the stage; but I translated it as a text to be read, and it made a powerful radio play, like plays written for radio by Günter Eich and Peter Weiss I also translated, when what was our Third Programme still had a use for this 'elitist' minority medium, an acoustic one in which poets have excelled. Again it is in Germany that this medium still flourishes, in the teeth of television, which once seemed to threaten it with obsolescence – for how much longer is uncertain, when resistance to the junk and advertising culture may be crumbling even in that so Platonic (Egghead) Republic.

Despite the hints I have dropped here, I don't know and don't care whether or not some foreign residue characterizes my work as a whole. As I write this I have received an article on my work – in German – quoting me as having distinguished between phases in my writing, one of mimicry, imitation of models, the next of 'word-scepticism', a certain distance between the matter communicated and the words chosen. All learning, of course, is imitation of one skill or another, and very few poets indeed seem to have come into their own without an apprenticeship of imitation. Foreigners, it's true, are supposed to be recognizable by the meticulousness of their way of speaking. But poets, too, pick their words if they aren't out for automatic writing or an indiscriminate spontaneity; and, if they try to write prose that is accurate, they will be picking their words also, often with the many 'buts' 'ifs' and 'perhapses' for which Eliot was notorious in his essays. Eliot was not as blatant an expatriate as Conrad, Joyce or Beckett, yet in his time the great divide between American and British English, American and British attitudes had already opened.

Reading two posthumous volumes of text by Paul Celan now – his correspondence with his devoted friend and searching critic Peter Szondi, and a collection of miscellaneous prose drafts and notebook jottings – I am struck by two things, other than by the fact that such books can still appear in Germany, meticulously edited and annotated. One is the confirmation in both books of the damage done to an incomparable poet by malicious and fabricated accusations of plagiarism. (These had already been fully documented in a separate study.) At times Celan could dismiss this campaign as the psychopathic phenomenon it was; but subliminally it precipitated his own paranoia, when a demented widow's charges were taken up by accredited critics and academics, rubbing poison into the wound inflicted on him by earlier persecution and the murder of his parents in concentration camps. The campaign began with the appearance of his first collection of poems in Germany and continued even when he had been driven into breakdown and suicide.

The second is reflections on his own poetry, and so on the paradox that poetry shares a medium, language, with many other forms of communication, but not with their functions, which it may find necessary to subvert; in his own case, an insistence on the essential darkness that was not obscurantist, for all the scientific and esoteric allusions in his poems, and not hermetic, since he never ceased to hope that his necessarily cryptic messages could be received. His poems were a groping in words for what he could not know before the poem found it, becoming not his but anyone's. Once the poem was finished, its author might not be able to elucidate it at all without betraying the darkness. Hence Celan's refusal to provide clues in the form of notes. Any one poem's itinerary could be neither retraced not repeated, preoccupied as a poet must be with the next poem's groping in the dark, up to the final silence.

Mutatis mutandis, this accords with my experience, with what Keats meant by the 'negative capability' of poets and with the doubt built into the vocation itself so startlingly voiced by T.S. Eliot, a poet seemingly much more deliberate, more self-assured than Celan in his public stance and pronouncements. It has a bearing, too, on why, ever since Plato, the place of poetry in any *res publica* – not least one as philosophical and ideal as Plato's – has been suspect; and why many intelligent persons have no use for its processes.

But it is in classical Chinese poetry, produced over a period of some two millennia, that poetry's imperviousness to social and political change is much more conspicuous than in any Graeco-Roman or Judaeo-Christian tradition. Wars, massacres, upheavals of dynasties, even the differences between successive religious creeds were intimated here and there by these poets – most of whom were civil servants when they could not or would not retire from public affairs – but not so specifically as to constitute a record of systems or events, just as the individuality of these poets was subordinate to their continuity – and the continuity of human life as such among the ten thousand things.

Another laconic revelation in Celan's previously unpublished jottings is his remark that he had learnt more from the work of W.B. Yeats than from the surrealists always included among his antecedents. This, too, rang a bell for me, recalling a time when a critic wrote that I was 'ghosting for the ghost of Yeats' – not without justification, at that formative stage of my work; but it would hardly have occurred to anyone to connect Celan's work with Yeats's, since the affinity was not one of manner, diction or form, but of what Yeats called 'heart mysteries'.

The Russian poet Tsvetaeva once remarked that all poets are Jews, probably meaning not their stubborn clinging to a minority faith and identity – the alternative to assimilation that has led to the present cruel impasse in Palestine – but that they remain classless, never wholly accommodated or uniform. What counts in the end is not how we are labelled and classified, least of all by ourselves, but how we have coped with the identities partly imposed by circumstances, partly assumed by positive and negative responses to the circumstances. Whether we accept the Fall as a dogma or as an incontrovertible myth, that separation from non-human nature gave each of us a measure of freedom and choice in the matter of who we are and aspire to be; but the judgement of how far the things we have done and made accord with the aspiration is not ours, and by writers must be left to critics as fallible as they are. This is where an egregious mug's game may link up with the human condition.

Mary-Ann Constantine
'To let in the light': Gwyneth Lewis's Poetry of Transition

O edrych yn ôl rwy'n beio'r cyfieithu – 'Looking back, I blame the translation'. So says the Poet in one of several confessions to Detective Carma, who is investigating the death of the Welsh language in Gwyneth Lewis's 1999 collection, *Y Llofrudd Iaith* ('The Language Murderer', 1999). Robert Minhinnick chose the line as a peg on which to hang the preface to his translations of six Welsh authors, *The Adulterer's Tongue* (2003). For him it was a challenge and a warning of the dangers of negotiating the painfully unequal relationship between English and Welsh through translation.

The line quietly disappeared in Lewis's English version of the poem, published in her next collection, *Keeping Mum* (2003). Its vanishing, she says, was not deliberate; but it is tempting to find an unconscious reason for its absence in the fact that the phrase was attributed, incorrectly, to Gwyneth Lewis herself, rather than to the self-dramatising Poet of the sequence. The Poet, after all, is a bit of a case, doing languages like drugs, reeling off a list of her addictions – a quick drag on English behind the sheds at school, the *frisson* of a German Umlaut, an overdose on Proust – and remembering her mother's purist rage: 'a language, she screamed / should be for a lifetime'. But she is one voice among many, and her promiscuity is no more the reason for the death of her mother-tongue than the quieter activities of the others, all of whom (archivist, farmer, neighbour, butcher, the detective himself) are implicated in the murder.

Lewis in her own voice is more serene about translation, seeing it as a fundamentally enriching process. Ten years ago, in a special Welsh-language issue of *MPT* (1995), she wrote vividly of her relationship with her two languages, of their delights and differences, of how they 'exercise on each other a kind of magnetic mutual attraction and repulsion'. A useful period of exile in America helped her come to the conscious decision not to choose between them, and since then she has written in whichever language has offered itself: the result to date is three volumes in each (Bloodaxe publish the English poetry, Gomer the Welsh). This year – and it must have felt like a kind of ratification of her decision to remain bilingual – she became Wales's first National Poet. But while Lewis enjoys and makes use of the invisible tug of one language and poetic tradition against another, she is not particularly interested in self-translation, which she finds: 'like trying to lift oneself up by one's bootstraps'. For this reason *Keeping Mum* is not an English mirror held up to its earlier Welsh incarnation, but a rapid series of snapshots of a book that was already very filmic.

Language and its loss are the intelligently-explored themes of these most recent collections, from the distance and desiccation that comes with recording a vanishing speech (the archivist daughter notes down interesting words for 'to die'), to the physical impact of that death on the community: in 'Y Gymdeithas Wledig' (translated below), the words are essential to the things they represent in such a way that their loss actually *is* the dissolution of a way of life (a translator's nightmare, since words like *eisteddfod* and *cymanfa* really need a short story apiece to explain them). Elsewhere Lewis carefully pulls words and objects apart to explore the gaps in between: in the deceptively simple 'Aphasia', the speaker's loss of control over the names of things describes a bewildering loss of self, but also reminds the reader how random those connections (although felt viscerally, and written into us from the beginning) really are. The Welsh and English versions of 'Dechrau'r anghofio'/'What's in a name?' play slightly different games with the notion that language is 'only' a signifier, that the wagtails and magpies will continue to exist without us naming them in our mother-tongue. Both finish with an image of swallows, the lyrical Welsh holding on to the thought that their cries are beyond language –

> Mae eu cri
> yn rhan annatod
> o'm henaid i,
> sŵn ei hoen
> yn ddyfnach na ieithwedd
> neu ddistawrwydd, neu boen.

[Their cry is an indissoluble part of my soul; the sound of their joy is deeper than language or silence, or pain]

– while the English is grimmer and more abrupt:

> There's been a cull:
> *gwylan*'s gone and we're left with gull
>
> and blunter senses until that day
> when *gwennol*, like swallow, might stay away.

Pure communication is at the centre of what matters (the swallow's cry goes directly to the heart), but the loss of a name does, after all, represent a diminution in the ecology of the world's languages. As Lewis herself puts it in her preface to *Keeping Mum* (and the wry smile is also typical), 'if endangered plants offer cures for cancer, what essential directions might be hidden in obscure Welsh proverbs about never ploughing at a run?'

But loss is not just about heartache; it is sinister, sometimes violent. In 'Welsh Espionage', a sequence from Lewis's earlier *Parables and Faxes* (1995), the encroachment of a second language is figured as a troubling loss of innocence, as a father secretly teaches his little daughter the English words for parts of the body. In *Y Llofrudd Iaith* the Poet remembers a childhood game gone wrong, when a new girl to the village, who had not learned Welsh, suddenly began to strangle her for real: she recalls a sense of detachment from her own imminent death, the bruises which marked and still mark her neck. Robert Minhinnick is quite right to be running scared: being a bilingual poet in Welsh and English is not like balancing English with Spanish or Russian. Although the forces killing Welsh are global and economic and often invisible, the spread of English remains the most obvious measure of its sickness. Having the status of a national language (as a glance across to Ireland will show you) is no guarantee of survival. Indeed, one of the side-effects of public bilingualism in recent years has been the slow permeation of the language by officialese, producing a Welsh calqued onto English jargon in a way which, for all the glossy independence of its lexicon, actually restructures the language at the deepest level: not so much translation as a transfusion of poisoned blood. (What that jargon is doing to English itself is another, and equally urgent, question.) No one working in two languages under such circumstances can do so in all innocence. Small wonder, then, that some writers make a conscious decision to stay in Welsh (and Lewis has been blamed in the past for not doing so), while others, like Twm Morys, have memorably refused to be translated altogether: 'Whenever I've seen pieces of mine in English, I've only dimly recognized them, like friends who've been in some terrible accident' (*Poetry Wales* 2003, 38: 3).

And yet the characteristic note in Lewis's poetry is not bitterness or guilt. Her work is not riven by duality; you do not come away from her books feeling bleak or hopeless. This has, I think, besides her innate humour, something to do with an ability to transform loss into movement. The poems are full of moments describing a crossing or a carrying-over between two states. The opening sequence of *Zero Gravity* (1998) intercuts an astronaut's voyage into space with a relative's death from cancer and the passage of a comet: 'my theme is change,' writes Lewis, 'my point of view / ecstatic'. In 'Ton' (*Cyfrif Un ac Un yn Dri*, 1996) the speaker is swept up by a huge wave and pulled down unconscious into the sea to be thrown back transformed – 'yn berson newydd sbon/allan o'r tryblith' ('a brand new person / out of the confusion'). In the sequence 'Cyfanedd' (translated by the poet as 'Wholeness' in *MPT* 1995), a nineteenth-century baptism at Llanbadarn transforms the River Rheidol into the River Jordan, an epiphanic realisation of that curious double-mapped existence led by so many Welsh villages – Bethel, Bethesda, Salem, Babel – in the world and in the Word. 'Dymchwel'(translated as 'Toppling the Wall'), from the same sequence, begins with a marvellous image:

> One morning the penny of the sun
> melted a hole in the pane of the sky.
> The light from over the other side
> spilled through and the men who were mending the road
> started to argue about tunnelling through
> to the room beyond the weather . . .

The hole gets bigger in the 'melting ice of the sky', and people gather spontaneously; working in groups to open it up. Light floods in, coloured birds fly through, and the people, masses of them by now, collect up their possessions and their children and walk through; the soldiers sent to keep order abandon their radios and cars. It is pure parable, a beautiful answer to one of the most desolate moments in Welsh literature, when, in the medieval story of *Branwen*, the opening of a door breaks up the blessed oblivion of the few survivors of the war in Ireland. Pure parable, except – and the English title confirms this – that we have seen it happen, on television, in our own times, in velvet revolutions and in the breaking down of walls. It is the tender attention to detail (the man lifting his child through the gap, the radios left behind talking to nobody) that makes this as much a political as a religious poem. Its radiant opening finds a darker reflection in 'Panic Attack', a poem from the second sequence in *Keeping Mum*, which turns the investigation of the loss of language into an exploration of lost identities in a psychiatric ward:

> You've fallen through ice. Above you men
> with ladders are sidling to where you fell in
>
> to this cold cathedral with its shattered dome.
> Ice has you in its picture frame
>
> for a full-length portrait but minus breath.
> Light doesn't help. Safety's underneath,
>
> a little deeper, if only you dare
> look up to the jagged dark. That's air,
>
> shouts, dogs barking, warm hands and ropes.
> Aim for the dark. It's your only hope.

The image of breaking through to another element is the same, and both mean salvation. As many people have noted, herself included, Lewis is a 'religious poet', but she is not one to turn her back on the world: her expressions of faith, focused as they are on moments of crossing over, do not leave unbelievers stranded. The angels that liaise between the different levels of being in the third section of *Keeping Mum* are not above manifesting themselves in 'stuffy rooms/smelling of cabbage'.

Lewis's great gift, then, is for capturing the transition from one state to another. The second poem given here, written for the opening of a new national museum in Swansea, takes the theme of industry and does precisely that. It is a celebration, though not an uncomplicated one, of the processes of work, from the transmutation of minerals to the transformation of lives. The piece is, on the one hand, a neat demonstration of the often-noticed fact that in Welsh tradition poetry composed for public occasions is an unembarrassed affair, a matter of craftsmanship (a fact which, incidentally, relieves the job of being National Poet for Wales of much of the cringe-factor attendant on becoming Poet Laureate in England). On the other hand, in all its brightness, it brings to mind the preface to the King James Bible, which describes the task ahead in the glowing metaphors of everyday acts: 'Translation it is that openeth the window, to let in the light; that breaketh the shell, that we may eat the kernel.'

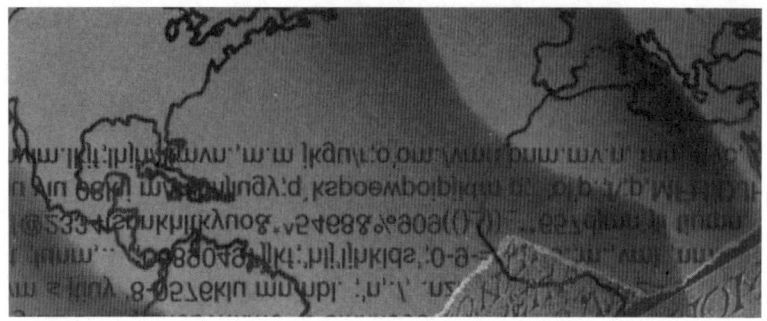

Gwyneth Lewis
Two Poems

Y Gymdeithas Wledig

Gadawsant yr eglwysi cyn iddyn nhw ffoi
o'u ffermydd. Beddau mewn corlan rhag i'r meirw droi

ar hyd llwybrau'u hieuenctid, eu heneidiau fel gwlân
defaid mewn perthi. Y mae lôn

yn draddodiad. A phlwyfi'r ucheldir
yn ddiymgeledd, gan fod gair

yn fan cyfarfod, yn neuadd to sinc
yn gymanfa, eisteddfod, pwyllgor dan dinc

y glaw digymdeithas. Dyma ystyr diwedd aelwyd:
corff mewn iaith arall. Cyfieithu nwyd.

The Rural Community

They left the churches before they fled
Their farms. Graves penned in to stop the dead

From wandering the old paths, souls alone
Snagging like wool in hedges. A lane

Is tradition. Parishes stand exposed
On empty hillsides, lost for the words

That were places of meeting, zinc-roofed halls
For singing and ceremony, for slow counsels

Held under isolating rain. Now witness the hearth's
   disintegration:
A body in another language. Lust's translation.

[From *Y Llofrudd Iaith* (1999) translated
by Mary-Ann Constantine with the author.]

Amgueddfa Genedlaethol y Glannau, Abertawe
17ed o Hydref, 2005

Beth sy'n dyst i'r trawsnewidwyr?
Tirlun. Priodas gwres a mwyn
yn creu man cyfarfod. Pridd yn troi'n gadwyn
yna'n drafnidiaeth. Morwr ar long
yn paentio pluen i'w danfon i'w fam.
Tanwyr yn moli ar allor y fflam,

yn creu ymherodraeth. Beth yw cof
y corff am ei lafur? Cryd
cymalau, cromfach cefn mewn gwely clyd,

a chelfyddyd pethau – swn
dur ar ledr yn hogi min
ar rasal fy nhad, sy'n estyn ei en

er mwyn iddo eillio. Amser yn ffrwydro
fel metel mewn ffwrnais. Beth yw pris
cyfoeth? Bod yn brentis

i broses. Beth yw braint
diwydiant? Na chollir gronyn
o egni. A'r galon yw'r gloyn.

National Waterfront Museum, Swansea
17 October, 2005

What's witness to the transformers?
Landscape. The marriage of mineral and heat
creates a place for people to meet. Soil is a chain

then transportation. A sailor at sea
paints a feather to send it home.
Firemen worship at the altar of flame,

forging an empire. What memory
do bodies hold of labour? Aches
and pains, a back's bracket in a snug bed,

the art of objects – the sound
of steel on leather honing the blade
on my father's cut-throat; he stretches his chin

to begin his shaving. Time explodes,
red-hot, from a furnace. What's the price
of wealth? Being apprenticed

to process. And the privilege
of industry? That not one quantum
of energy's lost. And the heart is the ember.

[Translated by the author.]

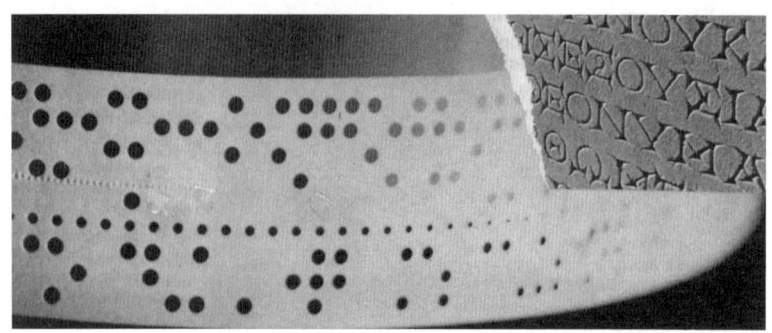

Choman Hardi
Switching Languages: a Hindrance or an Opportunity?

'What language do you dream in?' people keep asking me. This is meant to be an important indicator of my natural language, the language of my thoughts and feelings. The simple answer is, I never remember the language of my dreams. Does this mean that I dream in Kurdish? Maybe, but should this imply I cannot write in English or that I am constantly translating my thoughts when I speak and laugh and make love in English? It is possible but unlikely. I go through ups and downs with my languages. On certain days I feel fluent in four languages, I can hear them all clearly and sing them. Other days I keep slipping over words even in my native tongue, and finding the right word is a big struggle.

When I came to England twelve years ago all I wanted was to be able to speak and understand English. I wanted to be able to study philosophy and read poetry without having to use the big Oxford dictionary. I never thought I would write poetry in English one day. In fact I was a very young writer when I came and my poetry was developing while I was living in London. A few years on, when the majority of my friends were English-speaking, I thought about translating some of my poetry simply to share it with them. I was at university then and my friends looked at my poetry book and said: 'It looks beautiful!' I then translated a few poems which came out really badly. Despite the fact that my poems were simpler and more down-to-earth than most Kurdish poetry, it was nearly impossible to get it right. At least, this is what I thought at the time. 'Yekek bereda teparee, chawekani pir boon le noor', so one of my poems goes: 'Somebody passed from here, his eyes were full of light.' The word 'noor', which is an Arabic word, literally means 'light' and has led to the creation of another word in Kurdish, 'noorani', which means someone with the aura of holiness. So the literal translation 'someone whose eyes were full of light' does not have the implication that he is holy in a super-human kind of way, and this is an important part of the poem. My translations of my own work seemed bland so I decided not to try.

Over the years, through my education, friendships and readings, my English became stronger, more natural and spontaneous. Through reading contemporary English literature, my style of writing gradually changed, my language became simplified and my images more pinned down (I am still not sure if this is a good thing). On the other hand, the longer I lived in England the more I realised there was little understanding of the Kurdish situation in the Middle East and therefore no real sympathy. This realisation made me angry for a while but soon I became conscious of my position as a Kurdish writer in the UK and the responsibilities that came with that. I realised that instead of being angry, I could write in English about the truths that are so important to me and are unknown to others. In this sense switching to English happened on two levels, linguistically and politically. On one level I can say that writing in English was by choice, on the other, it was just a necessity. When I started toying with the idea of writing in English, there was a period when I wrote in both Kurdish and English. Most of the time the poem itself decided what language it wanted to be written in. 'Jamek aw ba dwaya birjin, beshkum zoo bigeretewe,' I wrote: 'Spill some water behind him, hope that he comes back soon.' This may seem meaningless in English but in the Middle East when someone goes away you spill water behind them so that they go and come back safe, like water. Such thoughts, words and idioms determined what language the poem would choose. Unfortunately, I now only write in English. Languages which are used more intensely have the tendency to take over like that. At times I feel sad when I think I may never write in Kurdish again. Other times I think that as much as English can claim me, I can claim it to tell my truth and give my community a voice. In the end, language is music and as long as this music becomes part of us, we can be creative through it. Also, we can recreate our identities in any language and writing in English may not be as big a betrayal as it sometimes seems.

Poet to Poet
The Scotland-China Project

Introduction by Polly Clark

The poems published here are part of a unique collaborative project between four UK poets and six Chinese poets which took place in both China and Scotland in 2005. The idea took shape when in 2004 when I was awarded a residency at Cove Park, the artists' residency centre in Scotland, to work with Yang Lian on translating one of his longer poems. I have no Chinese and Yang Lian had (at that time) not a great deal of English, but I had found from earlier study of his work in *Where the Sea Stands Still* that we shared many of the same artistic concerns in our poetry and, strange though it seems when I had so little knowledge of China and of Chinese poetry generally, we were imaginatively very close. Over five days Yang Lian and I worked through his poem line by line, image by image, using dictionaries and a French translation when we hit an impasse. Most of all we took time, as much as was necessary to talk through every aspect of the translation. It was very hard work, but the resulting translation was alive and true in a way that a conventionally delivered translation cannot be. Such was the success of this that we decided to offer the process to other poets, who might also discover that the sympathetic imagination can transcend almost all the difficulties of language. In June 2005 four UK poets went to China to meet their Chinese counterparts and begin the process of pairing up and translating. In September the Chinese poets came to Cove Park in Scotland to spend a further week working together. The project has been a creative turning point for the poets, demonstrating the unique power that the poetic imagination has to open one culture to another, and to reveal what is true in both.

More details about the project can be found on www.pollyclark.co.uk

Translations and comments by the translators

Antony Dunn: Comments on 'Monster' by Xi Chuan

The most immediate challenge of Xi Chuan's poem was its sheer scale – a monster indeed. This version – and it really is a version rather than a translation – has been distilled to around a tenth of the poem's original size. It was clear from the start of our discussion that the 'monster' is an embodiment of nameless fears, but trying to get to the real heart of it led us in extraordinary directions. Xi Chuan wrote this poem in the aftermath of the cataclysmic events in China in the late eighties and early nineties, when a widespread collective depression struck an enormous number of the population – particularly, for some reason, young people of Xi Chuan's age. So, on top of all the usual linguistic and literary challenges of translation, we were dealing with a very painful collision of political and personal histories – something inherently difficult to talk about. But it was a genuine privilege to be given access through this poem to events which rocked the political, cultural and personal life of China, and the world, so violently.

'Monster'

I see it coming, panting with bad news,
ashamed of where it's been and what it brings
and how it somehow can't recall a thing.
It gathers us up quietly, by ones, by twos,
avalanching into town – somewhere new
to find someone to get its teeth into –

Hell I feel like a bird looking for a flock
in a field of scarecrows . . .

It hates me, for sure, from haircut to heart –
the mourning, the caution and all that broods
in the fakery of my lighter moods.
It'll squeeze through this dead-locked door and start
to smash up my place from mirror to blinds;
all the stuff to stuff a life behind –

Listen to me; I'm spouting guano here –
a sea of guano . . .

Let's call a spade a spade to give ourselves
a handle on the thing – without a name
the monster's fleshed and dressed in mist – and tame
the cloud of it until the dark resolves
to something we can get our heads around;
the dread of all we love gone underground –

What if I'm the cock clawing his bloody life out
from under the pit of beaten friends . . .

Our monster will not have you turn its head
with all your bling – it couldn't give a squib
for your ride, your chick, your million-dollar crib,
your politics, your place, your faith, your bed
of stinking roses – it's locked onto that bit
that knows even a vacuum can turn to shit –

*Oh, somebody, please, give me wings to put a thousand miles
between me and all this squawking about myself . . .*

The poor creature wouldn't know its own face
in a mirror shop. It follows you, lost
as a lover, then eats you for breakfast.
Over and over it wakes to the taste
of the bender, the binge it's forgotten.
Hair of the dog. Sleep-walk. Again. Again –

*Come on you chicken – get some pavement blood in you.
Get on with it.*

W.N. Herbert

Comments on 'A Night in the Purple Palace (Adagio)' by Yang Lian

My friend Brian Holton, who has translated several books by Yang Lian brilliantly, was most recently working on the book from which this poem comes. He commented to me that, not only were these the first erotic poems published in Chinese since 1911, but, 'the bastard is using rhyme!' To be precise there is a single recurrent rhyme throughout the poem, alternating with unrhymed lines, but I now know exactly his combination of frustration and affectionate admiration. Having chatted with Brian about previous translations of Yang Lian's work, I knew what I was letting myself in for. His long lines combine extraordinary images and evade all sense of the succession of moments in favour of a timeless zone; he moves rapidly between an intensity of perception and an intensity of sensibility – everything that delighted me as a reader would, I know, torment me as a translator. And yet I have enjoyed few creative jobs more in recent years – that close proximity of difficulties and joys perhaps explains why translation is second only to creation: the interrogation of your own inspiration translates directly into confrontation with the text and here (uniquely) dialogue with the translatee. The rhyme was relatively simple – I knew such long lines would mean half-rhyming couplets would have a muted effect not unlike the original. But that last line caused endless grief: because Chinese can be more elastic about the way it indicates subject and object, it took me ages to come up with a phrase that clearly stated the unusual: that it was the word which rested in the speaker's hands. As for the eroticism, it seemed to me that a sly and self-deprecating humour came through the poem that I tried to catch in the double entendre of the universe's wink.

'A Night in the Purple Tulip Palace (Adagio)'

In this seraglio night always consists of   moonlight, jade steps and a curtain of pearls
all imaginary   a bunch of flowers against blue wallpaper
imagine   caving in under the concubine's clothes a mound of snow
snow waiting impatiently to be possessed   its crystalline body slowly
turning   constantly curling in on itself in a slow dance
a bunch of tulips divesting itself of the love of self as it brightly declines
a kind of purple whisper   which must be spoken breathily
addressing only him   as he crushes the petals heavily
a drop of purple milk   like a concubine impatiently waiting to be sucked
concentrating   the entire world into one burning duct

In this seraglio   fire always has the rude playfulness of tongues
a pointed tip   licks the emptiness of skin   midnight's cling
green like leaves gathered at the concubine's ankles
his preference for her   a shower coming from every angle
watering the flower   the little purple bowl of her nipple fills
in revenge against time   the pigment holds ocean's deepest spoils
a bunch of tulips slips in a single night from soprano to mezzo

tonight   tyrannous beauty is balanced by this aesthetic of
   erosion
this evasive scent which the concubine keeps for him alone
   and only lets him savour
when the silky light can't stop   purple very gently splays
   open

In this seraglio there's always this dead bone phosphor light
   becoming a pistil's gleam
conducting the body's desire   to be played for all four
   seasons
carving out this hole cut through   the concubine's
   sculpted days
the wallpaper is blue like a crazy mind sewing up all past
   pains
only once   the hours' bitemarks into each flower
darken endlessly   the night is stitched onto flesh
   endlessly fresh and tender
once in the beginning   purple   gradually spread like a
   drop of milk
slowly absorbed by the universe   which sees his
   lasciviousness   and winks
by staring he bestows on the concubine a totally dark
   grammar
the vase is like a word resting between the hands

Comments on 'Nameless Lake', by Zhou Zan

Zhou Zan was one of the Chinese writers whose work I only became acquainted with because of this project, and it has been a revelation to hear not just a younger voice, but a female voice, in a poetry that can feel dominated by its elder statesmen. Her poems rotate around quiet gestures that, with a little knowledge of their cultural background, can have profound consequences. Here I was intrigued first of all by the title – to leave it in the Chinese (Wei Min Hu) would not carry the charge it has as a phrase. Zho Zan explained that it is a small lake in the campus of Peking University, and it is also the name of a student magazine. But that is only to touch upon its many associations. During the Cultural Revolution, she said, professors and students alike chose to commit suicide by flinging themselves into it. Obviously these were facts which, if I had allowed them into the poem, would swamp it, so I opted for a quiet yet enigmatic tone, and tried to keep things clipped. The last two lines caused particular bother because they have a beautiful, neat, and completely untranslatable effect. The penultimate line actually ends with two characters meaning 'accident'; the last line ends with the same two characters, reversed. This means 'story'. This couplet, it seems to me, contains level after level of meaning – not least the suggestion that an incomplete story always points to what remains untold, be that tragedy or the puzzles of the inner self. I knew I couldn't find an equivalent, let alone something as simple and elegant, so I opted instead to push two words together that had a certain visual resemblance: 'account' and 'accident' – a poor copy but mine own.

'Nameless Lake'

Now the roads that lead to you are stuck with signs
so any sense of exploration has totally vanished.
Luckily, the memories have been hoarded up,
perhaps they're locked in a desk.
Hurrying steps, unlike faces, can't be forgotten.
Some preferred to call the walk around you
'exercise' – this was just to keep in line with
the idea of education. Your surface once mirrored
too many faces, but didn't retain anyone special.
So when your tale is told, people think
that's not an account, it's an accident.

Pascale Petit

Comments on 'The chrysanthemum lantern is floating over me' by Zhai Yong Ming

Zhai Yong Ming lives in Chengdu City in Sichuan province. She made her reputation in China as a bold feminist poet, innovative in her gutsy depiction of women's experiences. Her first collections were influential to younger women poets, many of whom now emulate her. She has since changed her style, and 'The chrysanthemum lantern is floating over me' is an example of her more recent work, where she includes elements of traditional Chinese life and classical poetry.

We soon discovered we shared common enthusiasms – our favourite painter is Frida Kahlo, and we have both written about women's lives in a visceral way. We are also both interested in using the supernatural, chthonic power, and trance-states, in our poems. This poem draws on seventeenth-century Chinese ghost stories, especially Pu Songling's the *Strange Tales of Liaozhai*. Yong Ming speaks very little English, and I speak no Chinese, so we worked through an interpreter. For my final drafts I also consulted Zhou Zan and Yang Lian on finer points of literal meaning.

After just one session with Yong Ming, I could sense this poem's intense but delicate numinous quality, and that was what I most wanted to capture. Child-spirits carry a lantern painted with chrysanthemums into the poet's present life from the past. The lantern belongs to an elusive 'owner', and with it floats a high-born young girl and her maids. The poem ends in the present-day in the poet's room. I changed some of the literal sense – for example, the last line means 'rise from the ground', but I hope that 'rise into the air' works better in an

English poem. There is no strict rhyme scheme in her original but I wanted to suggest how she used half rhymes and chiming assonance from Chinese classical poetry to give the story a timeless feel.

'The chrysanthemum lantern is floating over me'

The chrysanthemum lantern is floating towards me
in pitch-dark night   in the enveloping silence
a low murmur of children on the riverbank
the lantern is so sheer   a bird's shadow shows through it

the children float over with the lantern
with their faint chorus
there is no fear   no play   no pain
there is only the lantern   the lightness of
   chrysanthemums
and the red glow of its candle

a young girl is also floating over
a young lady and her maids
their hair up
their luxurious clothes   nothing but
silk   ribbons and buttons
nothing but tinkling tassels when they walk
tassels   ear-rings   phoenix hairpins

the young girl and her wet nurse
have known death
they are both searching for something leisuredly
they face the moon at midnight
the young girl is gentle   and the light is gentle
they are flowing towards me
transforming the ordinary night
into a somnambulist trance

every night
the lantern flows over me
its owner   wanders to the end of heaven
his pace sometimes fast, sometimes slow
no one can catch up with him
the children grow up with him

this is the story of the changing world and of the lantern

if I sit on the floor
I am afraid of the power
of the chrysanthemum's shadow   the light's shadow
   and the shadow of people.
and I sometimes slowly, sometimes quickly
make a tinkling sound in my room

if I sit on the bed
I enjoy this sensation
I also feel I'm gradually turning transparent
changing colour
all night I merge   into mist
then rise into the air

Polly Clark

Comments on 'Pine Forest' by Zhang Wei

Zhang Wei is best known as a novelist in China, although he has published two books of poetry as well as his thirteen novels. His novels are often concerned with the land and with ideas of tradition and some of these ideas are part of his poetry as well. Zhang Wei has no English at all, and so we worked through an interpreter. He does, however, have an imagination with which I am greatly in sympathy and we had remarkably little difficulty in wrestling with the philosophical complexities of 'Pine Forest' despite our lack of language. The poem presented some interesting challenges: firstly, the Chinese have more words for big spaces than exist in English. In this short piece, Zhang Wei talks about the 'far distance' and also the 'broad emptiness'. Much discussion enabled me to show in English the difference between these two, vital for the emotional depth of the poem.

My other major challenge, which is still unresolved, is the beautiful image of nature's sounds being laid as 'squares' on the ground. Chinese characters are all based around a square, and in Chinese there are also five natural elements, each of which has a character of its own, and is often a 'side' of another character. The image is of all of nature becoming fragments of meaning upon the ground. I could have said this of course, but I so loved the 'squares' and would have had to change the line so drastically to incorporate the meanings that for now I have decided to let the image stand. I am still mulling it over, however.

Finally there is just a note: 'pagoda' is the actual Chinese word for a pine cone. It is so perfect for the poem, with its connotations of temple and mystery, that there was no way I was going to translate it.

from 'Pine Forest'

On the coast of Longkou there is a vast forest of pine trees.

Here is a land of sorrow growing, of mercy standing still.
In its solemn breath you can feel the questioning of the far
   distance
beyond seeing and knowing.
The arms of the forest reach forever into ampleness, into
   emptiness,
until the pagoda at the wrist grows and is full of prophecy.
The thick hair of the trees weighs on their heads, they stand
   with their hands low.
The fall of each needle can be heard clearly.
Here all the sounds of nature are cast into bright squares
laid carefully on the ground between the trees.
Here all the stories of the present and the past are bearded
   and stooped.
The earth is mute. Its bears its wounds and numberless age.
How many cruelties have been rehearsed and played out in
   this place.
How many grasses have been trampled and lost.

Antony Dunn

Comments on 'May Rose' by Tang XiaoDu

In suffering my attempt to translate it, this poem turned out to be rather like the vine-roses themselves – it clutches onto its secret with some tenacity. On the surface, it's a love poem to his wife on the occasion of her birthday, but unfurl the bud and it's also a kind of cultural warning from Tang XiaoDu to the artistic community of China. Written in 2002, it's written out of the extraordinary events of the late eighties and early nineties, in the aftermath of which many Chinese artists of all disciplines – according to XiaoDu – rushed to appropriate the most fashionable styles and techniques from Western cultures. 'May Rose' proposes that the greatest artistic achievements – the 'true fragrance' – will not be born of fickle and gaudy fashions any more than the love within a marriage can be rushed into being or effortlessly maintained.

May Rose
(For R.Y.)

Of course, this is a secret —
how the trysting vines
have snatched the spring
from the armoured branches

but, not knowing how to undress it,
clutch it with a secret strength
this way, the winter through,
tense the veins of themselves to blue.

While snowdrops bloom, then the cherry,
in turn the peach, the apricot,
this fervour keeps, buried and buried
to the indifference of snow.

Slowly! It must come slowly.
Endurance eases the weight of endurance.
No true fragrance will be too late in this world.
Look at these little fists mobbing the wind —

my flower affair like a million bombs
bursting all at once, at once.

Notes on the Chinese Poets

Yang Lian: Internationally renowned dissident Chinese poet. His latest collection *Concentric Circles* is published by Bloodaxe Books.

Tang Xiaodu: Influential publisher, critic and poet based in Beijing.

Xi Chuan: author of four collections of poetry. He was awarded the Modern Chinese Poetry Award in 1994.

Zhou Zan: Young poet and academic who has published individual poems widely in China. She is a specialist in modern Chinese poetry and has published books and essays on the subject.

Zhai Yong Ming: acclaimed poet in China with eight books to her name. Until now never translated into English.

Zhang Wei: well-known novelist and poet in China, author of thirteen novels and two collections of poems. He is also the founder of Wansongpu College, a writers' retreat in Shandong Province.

Antonella Anedda
Five Poems
Translated, with an introduction,
by Jamie McKendrick

Antonella Anedda was born in Rome in 1958, of a Sardinian family. The languages she was brought up hearing, however, were, apart from Italian, Logudorese, Catalan from Alghero, and Corsican French mixed with the dialect of La Maddalena, an island off the coast of Sardinia. Her three books of poetry so far, *Residenze invernali (Winter Residences)* 1992, *Notti di pace occidentale (Night of Western Peace)* 1999, winner of the Premio Montale, and *Il catalogo della gioia (Catalogue of Joy)*, 2003, and her two books of essays, are written exclusively in Italian, though in a recent interview she has remarked of her Italian: 'I could say that I write in a foreign language which I lose and rediscover at each new occasion.'

Her writing in Sardinian is of relatively recent date:

'It began after an operation . . . I can only say that at a certain time the sounds that rose in my memory were these harsh ones of a pre-scholastic language, thick with consonants and shorn of adjectives. And I understood my own Italian in the light of those sounds. When I translated (these poems) from Sardinian to Italian I saw that one language steered or guided the other and that most likely I had always "translated" into Italian from that language.

'I don't know if I will write other poems in "limba logudorese" [the language considered the most pure – that is spoken and written in central Sardinia], but this experience has involved a descent into "una lingua non bassa ma profonda" ("a language not low, or vernacular, but deep") which Luigi Meneghello speaks of.'

I think that also for the reader these new poems in Sardinian shed light on her earlier poems in Italian. From her first book with its insistently Russian subjects and atmosphere, a sense of otherness and estrangement has been a marked feature of her work, which has a slow, resistant, compactness of phrase – a poetry in which nouns are given great weight and essentiality, a quality of 'thingishness', or *Dinglichkeit*. What's most unusual in her work is the combination of a severe distance of perspective and an abrupt, sometimes searing intimacy of tone. Her new poems in Sardinian suggest that this particular combination may also involve an encounter between two distinct languages.

Contra Scauro

No ischio iscrivere de Roma in battor dies.
Meda belluria, dechidu, meda mutas 'e linu.
Forzis gòi – sunt binti seculos – pessaint cuddos sardos
bennitos a dimandare zusstissia contra Scauro.

'Zente chene ide . . . terra ue peri su mele est 'ele'

Gòi nàrriat Cicero in faeddu suo. Ora, in mesu petras
bortat suo lumene, lestru, minutu. Ma sicutera
morint sos distimonzos, s' ape tribulat.
Reghet su mele: limba 'e lidone, gardu et sale.

Name

How can I write of Rome in one or seven days
– a glut of beauty, taste and linen tunics.
Maybe those Sards, 20 centuries ago, felt this
when they came to plead for justice against Scaurus.

'A truthless people . . . land where even the honey is gall'

Cicero said in his oration. But his name, now,
tiny and rapid, flits among the stones, and just as
then, witnesses die, the bee labours on.
Honey endures – a tongue of salt, arbutus, thistle.

[Translated from the Sardinian.]

Note: In 54 BC, Scaurus, proconsul in Sardinia, was accused of extortion and of being the cause of the suicide of a woman he had raped. The Sards came to Rome to testify, but Scaurus had as his defence lawyer Cicero, who poured scorn on these unkempt figures, covered with animal skins, bewildered among the columns of the refined Tribunal. Although guilty, Scaurus was absolved.

Limba

Non tenes baùle 'e istrisinare in supr'e nie
Ma unu cane a trémula in s'iscuriù.

Limba-matre ses triste.
S'azu s'inniéddigat in sa sartàine.

Sa mùghit'anziat.
Sos ventos si coffundent.
Eolo survat et Babele s'isparghet.

Fiza-limba tràchitas a ghineperu.
Una tremita tua naschinde
est ch'astula de livrina in mes'a isteddos

et sas nues, sas nues a sa thurpas fughint
iscanzellande dae chelu onzi zenìas

Tongue

You own no coffin to drag across the snow,
just a dog shivering in the dark.

Mother-tongue you're heavyhearted;
garlic blackens in the copper pan.

A low drone rises from the hearth.
Winds tangle throughter all confused.
Aeolus blows but Babel's left alive.

Daughter-tongue: creak of the juniper.
Your shudder at birth's a shard chipped off
a storm among the planets

and the clouds, the clouds blindly race
obliterating from the skies
all trace of lineage.

[Translated from the Sardinian.]

Archipelago
(a collapse)

Red and grey; a broken crown of salt and granite.
A breeze seeping from the heart of the rocks.

I fell under the few clouds
one day in the full springtime
with a bush bent under my body
and the whole promontory at my neck.
I had sand in my ears, the dog's paw
uneasy at my temples.
A disturbance we know from dreams
the moment movement meets the enigma of space.

All the islands flew apart
recreating exactly the void between the stones
refuelling themselves with wind at every stop.
The boulders sprang off whistling
like slings as far as my frozen feet
and breathing was a bristling trunk to swallow
with eyes tight shut
as far as the roots.

At first there was the house, grey and perfect in the
    sunlight,
but out of kilter – old nails, a chair –
then that whistling interspersed with voices,
two children and a dog's tongue
like a touch of the infinite at my throat.

Perhaps it was this that showed fate
how the lifeline still burned in me
when the skinned hand moved
to crush a fly
aimed unflinchingly skywards.

[Translated from the Italian.]

May, La Maddalena Island. Dream Fragments

Against the arch of the mountains
the curve of your chest
calming my space.
Your slow commands within the dream, the voice
which said: 'Turn over, stretch out on this beach
as though you'd dug a bed out in the path.'
Obeying and finding peace by turning
while my spine bends, my body weighs
and you extend wild lilies on the sand.

[Translated from the Italian.]

April, La Maddalena Island.
Dream Fragments

Clear, but thickly strewn as we imagine
the Aurora Borealis
a scene of silent fish.
Water in ice. A cautious bait that's lowered.

(I blow on the Bocche, fly ahead over the rocks
on through the cold, across continents, to your house, to
the wardrobe's wooden heart, to that now
unknown and darkened bed.
Your face is the door's walnut arch
mine the dawn encroaching on the window.)

A figure wavers in the dream.
It's the drunkard who yesterday on the bench
was rocking and singing with his mouth shut.

[Translated from the Italian.]

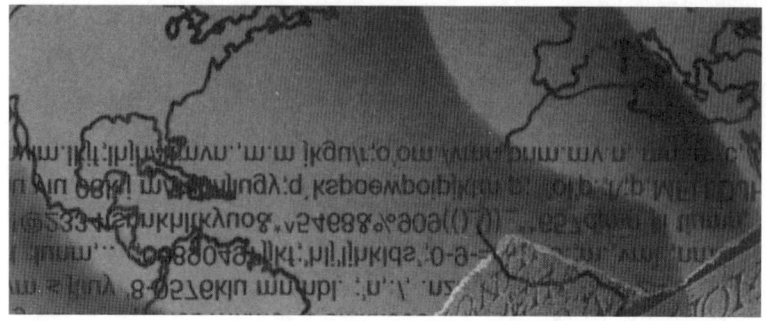

Dimitris Tsaloumas
Four Poems
Translated, with an introduction,
by Helen Constantine

If ever a poet could be described as being 'between the languages' it is surely Dimitris Tsaloumas. He arrived in Australia from the Greek island of Leros at the age of thirty and, as he writes in an essay first published in *Island Magazine* in 1984, 'set out to conquer the Antipodes and landed there in metaphorical semi-darkness. What little English I had managed to teach myself proved hopelessly inadequate and indeed quite troublesome, as nobody seemed to understand me, and it was a long time before I was able to produce intelligible sounds and to understand others when spoken to.' In that essay, reprinted in *Dimitris Tsaloumas, a Voluntary Exile* (Helen Nickas, Owl Publishing, 1999), he describes this linguistic, cultural and poetic journey: his childhood, largely deprived of reading matter, in the Dodecanese which was then under Italian occupation; his introduction to English literature via Dickens and T. S. Eliot and the impression made on him by the great Greek poets Elytis and Seferis in the years after the Second World War; his move to Australia into 'voluntary exile' in 1952, after publishing two volumes of verse in Athens, and the period of about ten years when he scarcely wrote at all. Tsaloumas started to write again in 1963 and went on to win various prizes, among them one from the Australia Book Council for *The Observatory*, a bilingual selection of his poems with translations by Philip Grundy.

The 'voluntary exile' has not been particularly easy for Tsaloumas. He has lived in a state of perpetual conflict, often attended by guilt and a feeling of divided loyalties, and has always given the impression of someone at odds with the society he lives in. His time is divided between Melbourne and Leros, but the discomfort he feels is not just geographical. It is not simply a nostalgic longing for Greece, for instance – although he is nostalgic often and inhabits a world that is somewhere in between the two places – but a sadness or distress at the direction society has taken, which is as much evident in modern Greece as in the New World. Recently he has referred to the 'corporate cancer eating away at the fabric of humanity and the planet's substance', a pessimism which is reflected in his writing.

He writes poetry in both Greek and English. We publish four poems here, three of them translated from Greek and one (in two parts) written in English. Like other poets who write in two languages, Gwyneth Lewis for instance, Tsaloumas has no trouble composing verse in his acquired language, but says he finds translating his own poems from Greek into English extremely difficult. How well is this phenomenon understood? It must have something to do with the sense the poet has that certain effects and assocations are quite peculiar to the language he or she has achieved them in.

Report

You asked me to let you know what I observed.
So here is the situation, though the meaning
Might have changed by the time you receive this letter.
I found him in bed, lying upon his back,
His eyes full of fear, full of suspicion
And rather larger than you may remember,
In a tangle of wires and tubes, suspended phials
Of slow-dripping waters, like some simulation
Of a hydraulic contraption. I said that as a joke
And he made as if to laugh. 'It is coming,' he said,
'Now all these storms are over', and through the window
Looked at the plane-tree alive with tender leaves.
Perhaps he meant the spring, but I changed the subject,
Said you had told me the news and how surprised
We were, that fine young man, that famous lover . . .
'You,' he said wearily, 'in your far-away lands
Go where the years go, but remember us
Who are left behind like flies in amber
Stuck here in time at the unmoving centre,
The roots that hold fast.' He smiled
His crooked smile and sighed. Then sleep took him.

Rain I

Lately there's been someone at my door
Or so it seems, a discreet tap-tapping.
But all my likely visitors have left
With the first rains. Sometimes I think
A southerly is trying at the openings;
Others I suppose it is only the rain,
The rain's particular cacophony.

Again tonight – until I ask, 'Who's there?'
And think I hear the answer: 'Me.'
I open – and blame my ears. Another time
Say who you are, my friend. I want
A clearer voice than the rain in the guttering.
Don't make me open my door again,
Without a word, only for the desolate night.

Rain II

Listen! Like a presence again
Outside my door, like a murmuring
This time, like conversation.
And I see my mother on the doorstep
And a forgotten brother of long ago.

Mother, we were lost, we were lost
But how tonight in such rough weather
And wherever did you find the child
In times like these, in such upheaval?
Not on the carpet with all that mud.
Leave your shoes on the step.

The child said nothing; but the mother found the house
Tidy; and she was glad.

Then we went down into underground places,
We lost each other on dark streets
While the sirens were sounding in panic
And I was pushing blindly at the doors of strangers
Feeling for my door in the dark.
But how can you enter without a key?
Who would open his door to me?
I sit here now and rack my brains
On the thought of that lost key.

[Translated by Helen Constantine with the author.]

Nostalgia

1. The Advice

Go back to the village,
I tell my brother;
the air's cleaner there,
the water fresh from those springs
in the rocks. Besides,
on their doorstep at dusk
the old folks will have one less
to sorrow for.
My brother's eaten up
with this nostalgia.

Untouched by the shine and hustle
of our great city
and its whirl of profit and use,
he moves as in a slow-motion dream
unmindful of gravity,
the way loose-haired maidens tread
on waves of hair selling shampoo,
or the way abstracted ghosts might move
in that sadness without end
of the Cimmerian dusk.

                          And yet
nostalgia's for the living,
my brother says,
feeds off the city's greed,
drinks from its thirst.
And it goes far,
travels beyond our village
to a place of gardens
and fruit that shines
in a cascade of old light and rots
in a splendour of setting suns.
Nostalgia's for the living,
he says, drinks from the thirst
of the dead.

2. Return of the Native.

This voice droned in my ear
all afternoon in the vast plain
against whipping rain
and a tangle of winds.
I'd been trudging along
on the road to the village
when through the wind-swept air
came the sound of bells,
vague as though muffled
in cotton wraps, from somewhere
far off.
        Yet I was there.
The bells were ringing vespers
up in the castle on the hill.

Indeed you are, the voice said;
the place is below, cowering
in the mist. Cross yourself
as you enter the castle.
The guards are unforgiving,
the knights forbidding in steel.
You look to neither right nor left,
pretend they are dead.
They are, but be on your guard.

So in the ruined old chapel
I light a candle,
pray for the old light to fall again
over the haunts of memory.

Pretend, the voice drones on,
pretend there's no place
such as you dream of
in our latitudes
under the known sky. There isn't,
but stick to stubborn faith
as you go down into the mist.

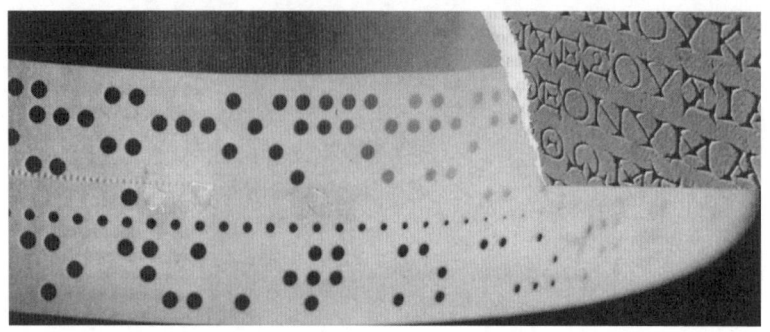

Mourid Barghouti
Extracts from *Midnight*
Translated by Radwa Ashour

These extracts are from a long poem in Arabic published early this year in book form. Montasaf al Lail (Midnight) is Barghouti's fourteenth poetry book. As in most of his poetry, he brings together the historical predicament of the Palestinian people and his own individual experience. At midnight, New Year's Eve, the protagonist relives scenes of his life which conjure up voices, faces, images and memories.

I

Now, on this earth which is not the earth,
I remember –
one remembers what one has never forgotten –
white bells
touched with the gold of morning
or were they the flowers

in the orange and lemon orchard
throbbing on their April branches?
You say: What's the difference?
I did hear a glittering resonance
which snatched me from my first school shirt
and invited me alone to the small orchard.
I went in playfully
when, all of a sudden,
the scent of flowers made me dizzy
and had it not been for my grandfather's arm
I'd have fallen in a swoon
of pleasure and death
(there's always an arm without whose help we die).
– Would oranges kill you?
Boy, what a disgrace!
He said to me, as if he said to me:
– Boy, you will know how to love a woman
and you will write poetry like Abdel Wahab.
– Who's Abdel Wahab, grandpa?
– He's the village madman,
he did nothing but poetry
and left nothing but poetry!
He said to me, as if he said to me:
– I'll always be worried about you.
The clouds were steps descending
from the centre of the sky,
the earth was of coffee beans and cardamom,
the wooden radio set
was the latest of inventions,
(it aired news we could not understand),
I rubbed the orange leaf in my hands,
I rubbed it in order to smell it
as they had told me to,
and before my hand could reach my nose
I had lost my home.

*   *   *

Life is hidden somewhere,
I know!
Life is hidden not far from here,
I know!
Shall I search for it
like a pin?
Like a broken button?
Like a ring in the dust?
Shall I go back to sleep for an hour
to see it in my dream?

Shall I go to mountebanks
and fortune tellers,
explain how it looks
hoping that a charm of their making
hung round my neck
might take me back to it
or bring it back to me?

Shall I put its picture up in police stations,
in emergency clinics
and newspapers,
with a sentimental caption:
   Life, we've forgiven you
   We shall not punish you for running away
   We are all waiting
Please life, come back!

*   *   *

Eternal runner,
running to it,
how long is the distance!

Whenever you're close to the finishing line
they push it back and move it away
from your tears of victory.

As if you'd been made of weariness.
As if you'd been made for weariness.
From the sun's doorstep to the moon's balcony
you keep wide awake when all go to sleep
afraid that the stars will fall
if your hands do not nail them
to the night's ceiling.

Calm down a bit,
rest a moment, friend.

Even the gods of ancient epics
leave their temples
haunted by the curses of oracles
and the deaths of heroes
and steal away
to have some fun.

Thunder
has its working shifts
then it draws its dotted blanket
and goes to sleep.

And like country women
bathing in the frivolity of water springs
the stream bed dries its body
with summer towels,
reclines on a pebble sheet
and basks in the sun.

To the ploughman, to the river, to the train
there is a time of arrival
and a celebration of homecoming.

From far away battlefields
boiling like a cauldron of bewilderment
the soldiers
return to the boredom of homely love,
thanks to rotation and their mothers' prayers.

The sun's weariness
settles into
sugar in grapes,
crimson in cherries,
honey in figs
and olive oil in jars.

War itself
leaning on its cane
walks a little in the corridors of peace.

Massacre keeps awake all through your night,
works at perfecting your absence,
then rests on its morning couch,
meek and relaxed,
it plays affectionately
with its friendly dog.

Clouds
with seams of burnt files
touched by the breeze of sleep
turn into satin pillows fringed with talkative lace
and playful butterflies.

But you, my friend,
were you created of marble we should have seen
the drops of sweat on your marble brow.

*   *   *

You hear the sobbing of your limbs.
I mean the song of your soul:

Life, life
even if you worked to death the mule of hope
under your thighs
before you reached its walls.

*   *   *

II

With a gentle hand, the storm reaches
for the handle of the world's door.
It gets in like a hesitant stranger,
strips off its masks one after the other:
throws lightning into woods,
darkness into torches,
despair into ships,
the devil into horses' hooves
blueness into the carriage driver's lips
and throws me naked
into the jaws of the night.

The storm
almost wrenches the stag's horns.

The waves' muscles
almost push back the coastline.

The sea is phosphorescent horses
whipped by unseen lashes,
they chew the drizzle, the horizons and the stars
and carry in their flying hooves
the smell of sulphur.

No boats are hosted by the sea,
the harbour is broken ceramics.

Nothing protects the trembling coast,
not even the foam's fur.

Two chairs on the sand
escape the storm
as if they were two lame persons
in a race.

The most efficient of tamers
will not close the jaws of this night,
he will not restore the loosened waves
to the guards' locks.

At once I take refuge in that house
with the imposing dome,
merciful arches,
warm blankets
and my grandfather's pictures
(worn at the edges
in spite of the solidity of their moustaches),
pictures secure on the walls

as if built into them.
My grandfather, still harbouring the illusion
that all is well with the world,
fills his countryside pipe
for the last time
before the advent of the helmets and bulldozers.

On the bulldozer's teeth
my grandfather's cloak gets hooked.

The bulldozer retreats a few yards,
empties its load,
comes back to fill its huge fork
and has never had enough.

Twenty times, the bulldozer
comes and goes,
my grandfather's cloak still hooked on it.

After the dust and smoke
had cleared from the house that had been standing there
and as I was staring at the new emptiness
I saw my grandfather
wearing his cloak,

wearing the very same cloak,
not one that was similar
but the very same.

He hugged me and maintained a silent gaze
as if his look
ordained the rubble to become a house,
restored the curtains to the windows,
brought my grandmother back to her armchair,
and retrieved her coloured pills,
put back the sheets on the bed,

the lights on the ceiling,
the pictures on the walls,
as if his look brought the handles back to the doors
and the balconies to the stars,
as if it made us resume our dinner,
as if the world had not collapsed,
as if heaven had ears and eyes.

He went on staring at the emptiness.
I said:
What shall we do after the soldiers leave?
What will he do after the soldiers leave?
He slowly clenched his fist
recapturing a boxer's resolve in his right hand,
his coarse bronze hand,
the hand which had tamed the thorny slope,
the hand which holds his hoe lightly
and with ease like prayer,
his hand which can split a tree stump with a single blow,
his hand open for forgiveness,
his hand closed on sweets to surprise his grandchildren,
his hand amputated
years ago.

*   *   *

Humanity has advanced a lot, old man.
Back is the age
of miracles:

Now it is possible
to obliterate
all proofs.

Now it is possible to prove
that what happened
never happened.

Now it is possible to prove that death
is the hobby
of the victim.

Now it is possible for the newborn
to start life
old.

*   *   *

How did you spot it? How did you spot it,
that single shining button over there
after clearing all the rubble?
The metal, the cries, the wood,
the bed sheet printed with camomile
about to bring forth its fragrance,
the dead bodies,
the yearnings,
the arithmetic notebook,
the tremor of the witnesses,
the taste of gunpowder,
the bones,
all vanished as if they were uncontested facts.

A single button
on a left-over scrap of material,
was it his coat's button?

Was it in her nightgown's tightly closed collar?

An extra button for the boy's shirt,
kept in the drawer, to replace the one

he usually loses
when he climbs the neighbour's fig tree?

Did it take her two nights to unbutton it
for her bridegroom?

It must have been his
and right below
on his shirt
the mark of an old bullet
which almost killed him.

Maybe it was in the blue quilt
that covered the blessed pleasure
of the newly wed.

Perhaps it was brought
by the lazy woman next door
who wanted her neighbour to sew it on for her.

Maybe it was in the shirt
of the young man who had escaped the shooting
and took refuge for two hours at their place
and died with the others.

At the hour of ash
when everything is silent
and the sun retracts his robes
to go to sleep
only the button remains
concrete and living
in good hearth
and almost ready
if you cared to bend down and touch it
to tell you what happened.

*   *   *

In this world's storm
my body tries to find me and I try to find it,
in this world,
where palm trees fall in epileptic fits
and minarets break up like chalk,
in this world
where truth is a wet matchbox,
in this world where the sponge creature
reigns supreme
not giving a damn
whether what it soaks up is clean or not
but is content with the grease of dining-tables
and the dust of chairs and shoes,
and does as it must wherever it is laid
and even when squeezed will not bother to get clean
but fills with a weight of air.

The voice says to you or does not say:
that's what usually happens:
some ships sink before they start their voyages,
some beginnings are ends.

*   *   *

There must be some other way.
There must be some other captain.
There must be a tougher sail.
There must be ships that do not founder twice.
There must be a way to live before you die.
There must be a woman to love and die for
without making the homeland jealous.

III

Your new day does not ask permission to come in,
it does not ask you if you're ready to receive it.
The day is impudent and selfish,
it insists on coming every day.
You hear its dawn climbing the stairs
before it breaks into your house,
the same way you hear them coming to arrest you
before they break the door,
before you rub your eyes,
before you're asked to have a cup of coffee there
with the hyena
with the gold tooth and the heavy make-up.

As for the birds,
don't they know that this is not the time for singing?
Here they are
singing
as usual.
They twitter melodies you do not understand,
maybe they repeat the echo:
Nothing equals
one more hour with you.

*   *   *

The day wanders in the streets of humans,
they do with it whatever they want
or it does to them whatever it wants.
but
when its face shines with sweat and exhaustion
and the pores of its sunset turn

like an orange peel the size of the horizon,
you take it to the emptiness of your room,
you settle your accounts with it
and it settles them with you,
it grows grey before you,
it grows old at the end of your bed,
it slips under your covers,
you think of it,
it does not think of you,
you are your own justice, judge and executioner
and it is not particularly good at paying attention.

When you wake up
you stretch out your hand:
The day is not there!
You can only see 'tomorrow'
roaming in the space of the world
like a philosopher who has lost his memory.
Overjoyed, the strutting dawn
steps in
to take up its new job
between two rows of swallows.

*   *   *

In a few moments
the sun leaves its bedroom
and in regal leisureliness
takes the thick bandage off the senses of the universe:

The buds wake up from their winter's anaesthesia
and they chat
intoxicated by their wine-red colours.
The flower prints on the girl's shirt come forth,
her heart learns its chiming,
her steps learn to take note

and her pillow yearns for her untamed hair.
The goats scratch the wall,
the light scratches the poplar leaves
blown by the winds,
it scratches the brass bed
and the bride's waist .
The soul of the universe
unfolds in the grass, the sage, the crickets,
the cooing and the dew,
in the strength of the mule,
the horse's lust,
the mischief of little monkeys in their cages,
and the wasp flies high
going astray in all directions.
The first pea leafs,
the turnips and the chicory of the wild
burst forth.
A wild love between a boy and girl
springs up
like the clashing of two stags in the drizzle.
The red stallion
turns on his back,
rubs his mane in the dirt,
kicks devils which he alone can see,
and he plays.
The stream rushes in its bed
washing out the difference
between pebbles and precious stones.
Bones ache again.
The grandmother takes her cup of tea
to the sunny triangle
near the porch.
Naughtiness gets restless,
the kids play their tricks on the good boy.
Geranium shamelessly parades its wantonness
on balconies.

The little chameleon
turns its neck right and left
like a proud fashion girl.
The ants quit their intelligent warehouses,
the snails get off their white castles,
coffee shops take their chairs out
to the pavements.
The swings
that stood motionless like sugar horses,
raise the children's laughter to the highest window.
The couple prematurely think
of silly names for their babies.
The widow who has experienced the patience of ashes
under the saffron of embers,
suddenly seeks her looking glass
and stands hesitant before her wardrobe.

But you,
with your wrist tied to a curse,
you are forced to follow up
what the swine of history
does to your day,
as if you have a sun of your own,
a sun that will not give you light
unless you kick it with your foot
or whip it with a lash.

From your cold stove, you take a piece of coal
and with a strong hand
you write on your wall:
I must have a day that calls me by my name!
I must have a home that is not this page!

Dear Fahimeh
Translated by Hubert Moore and Nasrin Parvez

The poem, originally in Farsi, is for Fahimeh Taghadosi, executed in Iran, 1982. The writer is unknown. Farkhondeh Ashena, who recently escaped from Iran, heard it when she was in solitary confinement, and memorised it.

Dear Fahimeh

That day,
that hot day in July,
when the Evin loudspeakers
called out your beautiful name and your lips
smiled, your eyes said to your friends,
'So today is the day.'

You went and your walk
was a perfume filling the corridor.
Everyone gasped, everyone asked with their eyes,
'Is today then the day?' The Pasdar
flung back an answer : 'Where is her bag?
Where are her veil, her socks, her money?'

A rumour went round that you'd given a sign
that yes, today was the day :
'I don't need my food,' you had said.

So tonight is the night.
A silence hangs in the heart of it.
Friends look at friends and tell themselves
that perhaps you'll come back.

Fahimeh dear, tell us, spare
a word for your friends. Is
the sky sad where you are, does it weep?
And the wind, does it ruffle your veil?
Back here, the ward sweats for your news.

And a message gets through :
wind-blown breathless dandelion
comes from the mountains to say that clouds
are massing up there and they're big with child.

Head held high, you are standing and waiting for this,
for the clouds to open, for you
to be mother of change.

Rifles crack.
The moorland holds its breath
at a star shooting across it.

It would be good to sing and go with friends
to face the firing squad, to dance,
to float in the rain.

In the long sea-silence,
a wave lifts, oars clip at the water.

A young fisherman bringing his boat to land,
rice-growers trudging home,
they shape their lips to your name.

Your name is beautiful for young girls born in July.

Sherko Bekes
Extracts from *The Valley of Butterfly*
Translated by Choman Hardi

The following are extracts from Sherko Bekes's book-length poem, *The Valley of Butterfly*, which was written in the late eighties, in the wake of Anfal and Halabja. During the Anfal campaign in 1988 three thousand Kurdish villages were destroyed, over forty chemical attacks were launched, 100,000 civilians ended up in mass graves and hundreds more died as a result of exposure to chemical weapons. The attack on Halabja, which was not part of the Anfal campaign, remains the best-known chemical attack on civilians in Kurdistan, partly because it was a town, not a village, where over 5000 people died instantly. Thousands more people who, during Halabja and Anfal, were mildly affected by the gas, later died from cancer and other diseases. In this poem Sherko Bekes, who was in exile at the time, is stunned by the world's silence towards these atrocities, he longs to go home and mourn the victims, laments the repetitive cycles of Kurdish history (continuous oppression and suppressed revolutions) and remembers and talks to other exiled Kurdish poets from the sixteenth century to the present day (especially Nali, Haji, Mawlawi). The book was printed in Sweden in January 1991, around the time of the first Gulf War. Following the uprisings in the Kurdish and the Shiite regions in March '91, Sherko Bekes was able to return to Iraqi Kurdistan a few months after his book was printed. He read this long poem to an alert audience over two hours. I first heard a tape recording of the reading in 1991 and even without seeing the book, I loved the poem and memorised parts of it.

Contemporary Kurdish poetry is a lot more elaborate than English. The abundant use of simile, metaphor, abstract and surreal images are important factors for writing poetry in Kurdish. In a land where tragic events take place in silence and where the difference in temperature between the harsh winters and blazing summers can be as much as fifty degrees, it is no wonder that poetry has to live up to and reflect these extreme conditions of life. Sherko Bekes has been a major figure in Kurdish poetry for the past four decades. Despite his sometimes difficult imagery and language, his poetry has been extremely popular. He is very much a poet of resistance and has politicised landscape, weather, birds and animals. In *The Valley of Butterfly* he switches from talking about himself as a person to talking about himself as Kurdistan. Certain expressions are abundant in this poem: 'the mountain of my head', 'the branches and twigs of hands and fingers', 'buds of tears', 'tulips of tears', 'beams of hair', 'rapids of their necks', etc. Sometimes his imagery is difficult to follow. For example, he talks about Nali's departure into exile in Istanbul, in the autumn rain. He talks about the rain falling on 'dislocated stone', which is a metaphor for what Nali will become soon – a dislocated man. He then goes on to assimilate this rain to tears and then to melting snow because the Shinirwe mountain (near Sulaimany city where Nali comes from) was burnt by bombs:

> The autumn rain of his departure,
> falling on dislocated stone,
> is the tulips of tears by the bank of Zalm,
> the song of snow on the burning Shinirwe mountain.

Another difficulty in translating this poem is that it is full of historical, geographic and cultural Kurdish references. Many personalities are evoked, from the exiled poets (Nali, Haji, Mawlawi, Goran) to the revolutionary leaders (Shekh, Xendan), religious leaders (Mawlana), historians (Hilmi), journalists (Jaladat) and famous lovers (Brimok, Las and Khazal). Often places, mountains and fields are linked with them. For example, in 'Haji's Kekon', Kekon is a hill near Koysinjaq where the poet, Haji, comes from.

Despite all the difficulties, I have tremendously enjoyed working on this long poem. Sherko Bekes has a few book-length poems but *The Valley of Butterfly* remains my favourite. This book evokes exile, flight, political persecution and Kurdish history better than any other book I know. This is why I decided to persevere and translate it. I hope that readers will become familiar with his language, style and frames of reference and learn to enjoy him as he deserves.

Extracts from *The Valley of Butterfly*

Drop by drop the rain writes flowers
as tear by tear my eyes compose you.
What streaming year of exile, what generous pain
that so calmly and stone by stone
bring to blossom the mountain of my head.
Branch by branch and twig by twig
they germinate my dried-up hands and fingers
and like pollen give me up to the wind of your love
to spring in the frost of your soul.

Crackling and rustling the wind reads the field
and gasp by gasp my breath grows your stature.
What green hurricane and what legendary
winged horse that from this end of the world
speeds to snatch and carry me away
to the distant winter quarters of your nomads?

Flake by flake, snow listens to the mountain
and word by word, my poems hear your love.
What yellow January and what blizzard
of story that so untimely
in the death throes of the day
like Braimok's love
field by field and mountain by mountain
starts me off towards you
through the path of white death?

It is a journey
it is a journey
a journey.

The journey of innate pain
the journey of a homeless tree
and the dance of a travelled wound
so I prepare myself.
It is a frost
it is a frost
a frost.
A yearly frost of the ill-fated spring
the frost of March.
It is the windstorm lamenting and the flowers sobbing
so I prepare myself.
When pain blossoms on stone
I prepare my horse, his head blazing for departure.
When the rain writes a greener poem
I prepare the whinnying thunder of these red clouds.
When the cradle, the shrubs
and the bush gallop
I prepare the colt of these restless white griefs.
When God is indifferent
and death perplexed
I prepare the *kejhawa* of pretty angels screaming for help.
When wedding means weeping
I prepare the earrings and dangling jewels of my
    lamentations.
When death is my bride
and poison is the world's present
I prepare the veil of this poem
and the necklace of this mist.

Twilight, after the *adhan* of your wounds I arrive, twilight.
Twilight, after your weeping dinner, I am with you,
    twilight.
When I come
light me a candle in holy Nali's summit
let it be the neck of a tree
or the finger of a narcissus

or the locks of a violet.
Light me a wound on the tip of Haji's Kekon
let it be the head of a decapitated poem,
or Wasanan's breast
or the figure of Halabja.
After the *adhan* of your wounds, I arrive.

When I come
carve me an arch
before the gate of your cold breath
one suitable for the king of sorrow and this crown of exile,
one suitable for Xendan's beard
for Jaladat's dignity.
Carve me an arch
by the buds of all your tears
by the leaves of all your sighs
by the oleander of your suppressed anguish.
Carve me an arch
by the red mud that you kneaded with your tears
on the grave of your loved ones.
Carve me an arch
by the square bricks of pain
of all your funerals.
An arch in the shape of Mewlawi's gently pointed turban.
An arch like the curved back
of Mewlana's retreat.

Don't bury those white flowers till I come.
Wait! Don't give them up to the cradle of history.
On the green grass of the hill
let them lie on their backs,
let them rest on the water's arm.
Let them lean on the wind's shoulder.
Don't close the sky of their eyes,
   don't cover them with a cloud on the mountain, till I come,
don't disperse them.

I wish, for the last time,
to wet my eyes with the spray of their perfume.
I wish, for the last time,
to embrace their breeze,
to put my lips on the lips of their desires, one by one,
to breathe in the disappointment of their chests;
like mother
and rain
and muskmelon
to smell them,
to pass my fingers
through the beams of their hair
and kiss them strand by strand.
Don't bury those yellow moons till I come.
Wait until I bring the moonlight of my exile.
Allow me to arrive
so I make the harvest of my poems
a belt for their waists.
I wish, for the last time,
to embrace the rapids of their necks
to rock their sorrows, one by one,
to climb, one by one,
the lemon-tree of their figures
poisoned in March.
To put my head on their snowy chests, one by one.
To bow to them, one by one,
to blow into the
holes of their wounds
and play the flute of their bodies, one by one:
(Hayran Hayrana . . . that is Sahar
those are the fallen eyes of Sahar
that is the autumn of Sahar's body
those are the scattered necklace-beads of Sahar's dreams
here are the hands, fingers and breasts
left behind by Sahar,
those are the planted screams of Sahar

these are the ashes of Sahar's paternal home
Hayran hayrana
it is hen-night
aman amana
it is dancing.)

Turn around and look!
How green is pain in the meadow of exile,
how succulent is this flowery torment
of this history of the country of disappointment.
There! Look!
How high is the summit of pain
in our dark chests, a flower at its tip.
Turn back! Look!
The snowstorm of the lovers parting
is blazing in the soul of the beloved.
Their tossing and turning is calm
and their getting lost is the path.
Look! How rows of pain,
chains of our high Kotal mountains
are looking over the fields of our love
one by one.
Look! Their burning is dance and flight.
The wings and feathers of their cry
are the drooping branches of songs.

That is the lantern of Nali's neck
burning in the night of the pacific sea
brightening the body of water.
He measures the depth of the sea by the height of poems
and sails his dreams at the bottom of the whirlpool.
Stunned by the whirling, the hummingbird of his fear
rests for a second. Over there
he lays greenfinch eggs for the winged fish of his poems.
Over there, he has colourful dreams about the eyes
of his homeland. He is about to drown when he reaches out

and takes the pearl of God's heart. He is about to drown
   when he
plants the seeds of sun and poems. It is only him
and his boat. Only him and the journey of dark waters.
Only him and the paddle of his pen, only him
and the bright sorrows. He is the vanguard
conducting the wailing of stateless waves.
He leads the wandering words.
Exile is soaking. The coast-less boat
rides solitude
and the garden of water
has blossomed Habiba's hair flowers.

The thirst of his love is thriving, raising the waves.
The path of his words is bright, they travel.
The autumn rain of his departure,
falling on dislocated stone,
is the tulip of tears by the bank of Zalm,
it is the song of snow on the burned Shinirwe mountain.
His passion is a piebald horse:
his calm is pawing
his neigh is silence
his distance is close
his *kiblah* is his country.

Istanbul sees him and doesn't know what lake
laps beneath the hat of this man
with his basil and snow beard.
It sees him every day and doesn't know
what grove and shadows
are within the valley of that tight chest.
The pigeons of the minarets and domes see him and don't
   know
what wings lie in the sky of that blue soul.
The mountain where the sun sets sees him and doesn't know
what ember, flame and fire burn

in the hearth of this exiled and wandering poem.
The rain and showers reach him and don't know
what roar, what pain, what movement and thunder
hide in the cloud of that deep soul.
The poor see him and don't know
what sobbing bread, whining water
and coldness of a lifetime hide
in the cottage of this old man's soul.
The lovers pass him by and don't know
what coquetry of sorrow
and what spring of vision
are within the dawn of those sharp eyes.

And that is Mawlana, the afternoon sun of the night.
He is the silent waterfall of God's heart and the porter of
   crying.
In the summer, the Indian rain falls in his eyes, in the winter
Sharazur is blazing in his soul. Every day
early dawn, the green-locked Barada disciple
concealed from the Amawi minarets of Syria
takes waves of divine light in a bowl of affection
to Mawlana's Sirwan lake.
At night he is the willow tree next to God's lake.
Daytime, he is the labourers' bread, its forehead burnt.
He is the mountain oak tree which walks every day
to the house of blaze and flame
and no matter how much he burns and shrivels
his branches and stems become more lush.
He is the snow mountain which of its own accord
goes before the just sun. The more it trickles
the fuller the pool of his sky affection.
At night, however much hell burns his body
to turn him to ashes and smoke,
in the day the vision of this pain is clearer
and the heaven of his soul, greener.
Mawlana, the phoenix,

kneads the ashes of his own body every day
to make a vase for God's love flowers
and puts it in the light arch above his head.

(Three holy statements in an unseen diary of Mawlana)

First:
a lover was put into the fire
but until his pure soul reached the sky and God's heart
he continuously played love music
with cords of flame.

Second:
You can plant your vision and it can grow
only if a tree becomes your lover.

Third:
I couldn't escape, your love surrounded me
now, in your new map, I am your island.

The other is Haji, the tree that chimes,
the windpipe on the lips of mountain's history.
Night and day, with the daisies of his eyes
he weaves flower knots and tassels
for the shawl of an orange tribute for his Koysinjaq
and the bleat of his sorrow's black sheep
is near Kakon and around the black tents.
He made balm from poetry
he made it his key, his dagger.
He made wheat and *adhan* from art.
He mixed words, perfume, screams and sunrise
into something unheard of, unseen, unsmelt.
In this grove of fear he has made poetry a tiger
who writes on the stature of darkness with his claws.
In his eyes homeland is the glitter of drops
of the homeless alphabet.

In this head homeland is the prayer-stone
in a shepherd's pocket, in love with Khaje.
In his voice homeland is the song of partridge
and laughter of two girls swinging
between two trees in a village.
In his ear homeland is the jingle of a beauty's anklet.
Every night, in the crying room,
he ignites a pink memory and a yellow poem together
with the flint of his head.
The water of his eyes like the water of Hijaz's clay jugs
is colostrum consumed by exile.
Daytime he is steam in Hijaz
at night he is a frozen lake in his homeland.

Over there, if the head of a stone
in Chinarok bleeds
over here he raises his hand from pain
and puts it on his head
Over there if a pebble gets stuck
in a river's throat
over here, one of his poems coughs
and touches its gullet.
Over there if a young song flies
over here, he becomes the sky.
Over there if love decides the hour
over here he becomes
a tree, a shadow, a home for the meeting.

From then, since the beard of pollen
stuck to the raspberry of exile
since Istanbul is shadow and the sun of homeland
has not shone on poetry,
since the wave of this blue winged water has flown
the gardens have been looking for him.
Since this cloud has fled
the mountains have been looking for him.

Since this Haybat Sultan has become nomadic
Kurdistan is distraught, waiting and saying,
When will this sun of mine return?

(An advising unpublished poem by Haji which I received
from an old, green-bearded stone years ago):

If this stone did not have strong arms
and his heart was not so tough
the wind would have rolled it over and taken it many times.
If that stone was not so sensitive
how could a seed brought by the wind
spill his chest open?

*   *   *

Long is the smoke from this grieved grove
like the figure of my map.
Long are the tears of these mountains and valleys
longer than Tigris and Euphrates.
Long is the smouldering of a blade of grass
as far as my wound's vision goes.
Long are the screams of this body's roads and streets
they reach God.
Long is the pain of my alphabet
from here till Khani.
It is long, it is long, it is long . . . long are my days in exile
longer than Europe's rail track.
I don't know what to tell you about?
I don't know what
I don't know
I.

*   *   *

– Is this poetry's left-behind locks
or the forelock of a village's dream?
Is this the broken mirror of a sunray
or of a girl?
And this killed river
was she the beloved of the field or a boy?
And this fallen scream
was it the scream of my mother or a tree?
Is this a nipple or a cherry stone?
Is this a burnt cat or my baby?
Is this my father's head or the nan-cosy?
Are these the fallen wings of angels or doves?
Are these my irises or olives and grapes?
I don't know how to separate them from each other
I don't know how to separate
I don't know how to
I don't know how
I don't know
I.

*   *   *

For a long time those villages,
muddy to the neck and wearing shabby clothes –
those rough-handed and -footed sorrows of my country,
were the embrace of freedom,
and the cradle for thousands and thousands
of fugitive hymns from my city's streets.
For a long time, the dribbling sweat
from the neck of their tired wheat and barley
was the reviving snow-water,
and a loving mug of *dogh* on the road
serving lines of stars on the mountains
and even the self-destructive flocks of wounds.
For a long time they were
the rosewater of anguish and every meal

from the dough of their own poverty
they made us nan.
They covered us with their sieve-like night
and with the trees of their figures, they made us shadows.

The embrace of these dusty-faced
barefoot and naked villages was our barn,
their conversation was our sweet Basooq,
their children were rhubarbs,
their elders, the stems and branches of the village mulberry tree.
They were the coughing mules
under the weight of our weapons.
They were eggs, cheese and onion
for our lives.
They were anklets and bangles for poetry
stories for the hearth of homeland.

*   *   *

Do you remember? That sterile year
you walked the waterless summer afternoon track.
The weapon on your shoulder was the shadow of thirst,
the coffin of a migrating death.
For you, for them, everything was the ghost
of a permanently ready fear, long and wide.
Sticks and stones, animals and birds, and even
the glittering eyes of a cat in the night
was the sign of death's call and ambush for everyone.
You descended the exhausted mountain
and entered the wound of the village:

When she came, she was a mourning pear tree.
She smelled of a very new death.
She looked like the sorrowful history of the mountain.
She showed you the head of her husband in her chest.

She brought you the crying milk of her baby.
She said to you:
– Why have you come?
What is left for you to come for? The sieve of our bodies?
Or bloody bread?
What is left? Why have you come?
Keep your weapons to yourselves!
Keep your revolution to yourselves!
Keep Kurdistan to yourselves!
What is left? What have you come for?

You drenched in a hot shame. When you turned back
you were dead! You took the same thirsty track.
You climbed the same exhausted mountain
and from the front the wind was angry,
it started with force and raised dust.
The whirlwind's oven reached you
and you got lost in it!

*   *   *

Now I listen to the muteness day and night
the muteness of stars and roses
the muteness of valleys and forests
to the silence and calm of ruins and ashes.
Now I converse with a deaf history
my tongue is a stranger to its own dictionary
my voice is a crouching skyless bird.

Deserted are the fields and valleys of this body
they were harvested
Deserted is the capital of this poem, it was smothered
Deserted is the country of this dream, it was burnt down
Deserted, deserted –

from this side of the wound to the other
from this side of the crises to the other.

You did not have time to pour Mawlawi a sip of water.
You did not have time to give Nali his shoes.
You did not have time to give Goran a spoon of medicine.
You did not have time, did not have time, did not have time.
You were autumn in your own place, without falling.
You blazed in your own place, without being deranged.
You became a candle in your own place, without burning.

(A message which is not rushed, neither is it poetry)

In the name of Halabja and five thousand moons
In the name of Mawlawi and five thousand flowers
In the name of Goran and five thousand doves,
for the brilliant scientists of Pushkin's country, Jack London's country,
Byron's country, Jeanne d'Arc's country, Bismarck's country.
The country of Garibaldi, the country of Van Gogh, the country of . . . the country of . . .
Thank you for the present which you sent through Baghdad,
on the morning of 16 March 1988,
to the flowers, the doves, the children and the poetry of Kurdistan.

*   *   *

You are standing on this boulder of hope.
You know it is unstable but you are standing.
(Stand as you are! A shaky hope
is better than the stable summit of darkness.)
This advice was written by the winy smoke
from all the vineyards.

Every time, I roll the mountain of screams and sighs
into the silent ocean of the world . . . but it does not stir.
Every time, I carry the decapitated head
of one of my years, one of my cities
and take it before the world so that it asks me:
'Where have you brought this head from?'
But it does not ask.

'If a gallon of my voice stirs
this ocean of the world's conscience will stir with it.'
This advice was given to me by a political barrel of oil!

*   *   *

A chain of proverbs, stone carvings and valuable sayings which spring from today's mountain, blood, smoke and failure.

One:
If the wind stands in your way
become a mountain.
If the breeze comes to greet you
become a garden.
(I read these words
in the newspaper of an oak tree.)

Two:
One morning in a cave
they chained a cold breeze,
in the evening, the breeze turned
into a windstorm in the valley.
(These words were inscribed
on the forehead of a black mountain.)

Three:
Is that a swallow flying
or the black and white scream
of my mother?
(These were the words of a child
from Halabja, half a minute
before he went deaf and blind.)

Fourth:
O dear God!
When will you visit Kurdistan?
(These are my mother's words every day.)

Five:
When a lover goes mad
he turns to poetry.
When poetry goes mad
it turns to God.
I am a lover and I am a poem.
(These were the words
of an exiled river.)

Six:
– How can he sleep
when he's killed so many dreams?
– He sleeps but he never dreams.
(This was the secret conversation
between two birds from a Kurdish city.)

Seven:
God and Kurds resemble each other:
both of them are without partner, without friends.
(These words were inscribed
on the wall of a mosque.)

Eight:
When you host the snow
make sure she doesn't get hot
so that your house won't be flooded.
(I heard this from an old fire.)

Nine:
A third of the landscape of my poems
consists of forests of hanging ropes.
(These were the words of a poet
whose life was too short.)

Ten:
I cut the mountain with my scythe
its scream reached God's crown
but when he dug it as deep as a weapon's length
for a trench, the mountain blossomed
and laughter sprung from its body.
(These were the words of an honest witness
of the war between Mazda and the devil.)

Eleven:
I fall or flower?
Between falling and blooming
I am a new season.
I am not the sun nor the shadows
I am a land
still looking for my face, colour and image.
(This was inscribed on the walls of
the Jasana cave.)

Twelve:
I will never allow complacence
to penetrate the clouds of my poems
so that even if I rain a thousand times
I think it is only once.
(A pen told me these words
which till its death was never without the rain of
  imagination.)

Thirteen:
You enemies!
Don't you know that I am a lake?
Don't you know that every stone which you throw into me
becomes a room for laying eggs of poems?
(These words are my only reply
dedicated to those stones.)

Fourteen:
You exiles!
We resemble the planks of wood on Amoon
we won't drown, nor will we suffocate.
But the saw of waves and file of coasts
will gradually turn us into smithereens
they will give us to the darkness of the ocean
and we get lost in it.
(These words were inscribed
on the headstone of an exile.)

*   *   *

16 March – before mid-day
a mad prince of modernism –
a mixed-race wind, mixed from the left and right
of the politics of this fallen world,
a wind, large-boned, ugly and arrogant
his mouth smelling of garlic,

suddenly arrived and started a yellow coup.
He confiscated the sticks and stones of the sky.
He became the only ruler
of this vast country of spring.
He closed the roads
between the sky and the earth.
He locked all the doors of heaven.
His voice a mixture of East and West
he read out his first rule.
In a space of time shorter than a leaf vibrating
shorter than water blinking
shorter than a lamb's bleat
he turned the angels, cherubs, birds, and the wingless
into candles without smothering them.
He made them into glass without breaking them
In the coast of the black water of that silent day
the groups of doves were white
but they did not coo.
In the green fields of this dizzy day
herds of horses were lying down
but they did not neigh.
Who can stand up
before this crazy air?
Who won't get confused?
From the Zoroastrian *gatas* to Marx's capital
to the swords of Zulfagar
they all threw up, blistered and then froze.
Bravery, heroism, fiery beliefs
they all froze in their trenches
before having time to pull the trigger
to shoot themselves.

*   *   *

Every time you lie down you feel
you have become a stone in the lovers' meeting place.
When you sit, you imagine
your head is a lump of clay
for the children to make things with.
When you get up you think
you have turned into a ladder to the roof of a village house
    over there.
When you sleep you feel that
you have become the dream of an oak tree over there.

My dearest!
This wandering moon of my love
has not come to this mountainous ember of exile in vain.
This rebellious river of sorrow
has not broken the calm face of water in vain,
it is not neighing with flamed screams
of the night and day of exile in vain.

My dearest!
For the sake of kissing a blade of grass
they cut the lips of one of my creeks.
Because of the flight of one of my poems
they turned clouds into a trap for me.
Because of a roaring wave
they suffocated one of my waterfalls.
Because of a neighing mountain peak
they nailed my valleys.

My dearest!
A pond went crazy when they deprived him of the moon.
The moon went crazy when they deprived her of the cloud.
The cloud went crazy when they deprived him of the
    mountain
the mountain went crazy when they deprived her of the
    snow

the snow went crazy when they deprived him of the land
the land went crazy when they deprived her of the people.

My dearest!
Now, in the thicket of iron, glass and concrete
my heart is a rabbit of the Piramagroon mountainside.
Now, in this misfortune of love
only the angels of your Gla Zarda
water my star-trees
and make the stump of my head flower.

My dearest!
Whenever it rains
I run and go before it for a few seconds
I keep thinking maybe this time, this rainfall
will smell of the Azmar and Goija rains!

On some days when the sun shines
I run and go before it for a few seconds.
The light lands on me and I close my eyes
And I keep thinking maybe this time, this sunshine
will resemble the sun on our porch and by our walls.

If sometimes the wind blows
I run and go before it for a few seconds
I keep thinking maybe this time, this wind
will be strong enough to lift me up
and throw some sand into my eyes
like the fast winds of Sulaymania.

From a distance, when I see a flock of girls
I walk faster and go towards them
I keep looking and hoping that maybe
a playful smile, a shy turning of the head,
looking from the corner of the eye, or blushing cheeks
will take me back to my city's streets.

Whenever I see a market
I run and go inside it, I circle around
I keep hoping that a fruit seller's calls
the fish seller's calls
the grocer's calls
will resemble the calls and screams of the evening market
by the pond, under our bridge, back home.

*   *   *

– Where do you come from? they ask me.
The same question becomes a raspberry
and makes my voice bleed.
For the thousandth time I name my flower.
Some of them nod after a second
as if a wind has run this past their ears once.
But most of them suffocate in silence,
their neck becomes an exclamation mark.
In desperation I take out a map from my pocket.
A map crumpled like politics
dirty and torn like the ethics of nation states.
I put my finger on my divided sun.
– From here, from Noah's ship I have come!
I was born in the snow of Judi mountain.
– 'You are still having colourful daydreams
daydreams from old myths and legends.
Your hope is a mirage.
My father too carried his homeland in his eyes
he was the palm tree of a coast
a sleepy coast in North Africa.
One day the ocean whirl chased him
he ended up in Oslo.
One cold night, in a bar like this one
he met my mother.

My name is Margarita.
Till he died, my father
had dreams similar to yours.'

These were the words of a half-Moroccan girl.
She told me this in a cold night
in a busy bar in Oslo. They were a grove of
cheerful girls and boys. They swayed
to the rhythms of music and songs.
I was sitting with a shy poem –
myself and the bird of my hallucination
myself and the smoke of my cigarettes
we were eating each other up in a corner.

The mixed girl, Margarita, has become
the moon in the snow of Norway.
She has become the steamy breath of these streets,
a letter in this language,
the wings of music in these bars.
Morocco, her father's country
is only three images in her mind,
three phantoms and nothing else:
a desert, a palm tree and a camel.

From that night on, Margarita made fear my shadow
a fear which counts every second of my exile
and brings its fog wherever I go.
From that bar on, Margarita planted a doubt in me
which has been eating my dreams up
and in the cradle of darkness
it carves out hopelessness for my coffin.
From that night on my youngest daughter's face
has become that of Margarita
her vision has penetrated my daughter's
her voice has spilt into her voice
the gardens of their hair are the same

and the colours of their emotions have become one.
From that night on I feel
my youngest daughter too
has been raised by exile
and like a drop of dew
she has mixed with the wind of this place.
On the night's dance floor
her body has lost her head
and every now and then she looks for it in a bar.
I feel that every day
a phantom comes and draws her picture for me:
The fading of her memories
the moulting of her language
the fall of her family
forgetting her father's dream
not being able to smell the breath of homeland
the melting of snow of songs
and her mother's stories.

From that night on I feel
that I too father Margarita
I have turned into a poem of a yellow sorrow
and one day I will set in the snow of exile.
Then, in another season
in a cold night like this one
in a bar, my daughter too like Margarita
will talk about me:
(My father was a mountain bird
he flew the mountain
and reached the snow of this pole
and one day here, as he was singing
his dreams froze with him.)

Notes

Kejhawa is a sheltered and curtained seat on the back of horses or mules for transporting important people and also brides.

Adhan is the calling to prayer, broadcast from the mosques.

Hayran is a type of Kurdish folklore epic.

Aman is an old word used in folklore songs, it is a sort of sighing for love.

Kiblah is the direction of the shrine in Mecca, the way Muslims face when praying.

Dogh is a yoghurt drink which is very popular in the villages.

Gatas are the Zoroastrian religious chapters, sections of the holy book.

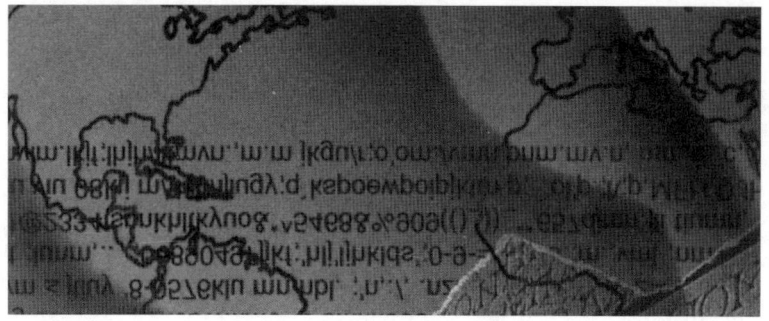

Ingeborg Bachmann
Ten Poems
Translated by Patrick Drysdale and Mike Lyons

Introduction by Karen Leeder

When a collection of Ingeborg Bachmann's 'unpublished poems', *Ich weiß keine bessere Welt* [I know no better world], was published in 2000, three decades after the poet's premature death, it caused a major, and often bitter, literary controversy. These were intimate texts that had not been burned by Bachmann, as had other private papers; but nor had they been released for publication during her lifetime. The family's decision to bring these pieces into the public realm, after so jealously guarding Bachmann's archive from academic scrutiny for so long, was seen by some as an important step in completing the picture we have of one of the most significant European poets of the twentieth century, but by others as an act of calculated marketing and a fundamental betrayal, encouraging posthumous voyeurism of the worst kind.

The hundred or so poems published in this collection (of which only eight had been published before) were for the most part written between 1962–1964, after the catastrophic breakdown of Bachmann's relationship with Max Frisch in 1960. Bachmann felt herself used and abandoned by Frisch and exposed to ridicule in his subsequent fictionalisation of the relationship in *Mein Name sei Ganntenbein* [Let My Name Be Ganntenbein]. The biographical reality is impossible to ignore and yet the poems are terribly discrete about the real contours of the life. Instead, they reveal the private moments of someone tormented by the desire to sleep and by hallucinatory dreams, obsessed with thoughts of death, babies dead or lost, fantasies of revenge, and despair at the lovelessness of the world. They are driven by a desire for obliteration and are greedy for anything that will bring it: morphine, alcohol, sleeping tablets, and desperate sex. But, more important, they are filled with mourning for lost poetry, the 'beautiful words' of earlier times, and a deep speechlessness.

> My poems have gone from me.
> I look for them in every corner of the room.
> Don't know in my pain how to write
> a pain, know nothing any more.

In truth very few of these texts could really be called 'unpublished poems'. They are sketches, drafts, versions, very many echoing the same images or lines, reworking them in different variations and forms, as she struggles to wrest language from the silence. Hans Höller's excellent 1998 commentary on just three of Bachmann's late unpublished poems reveals how obsessively Bachman worked through drafts before allowing a poem to be published. This volume too contains facsimiles of the manuscripts which show the increasingly frantic handwriting, the gaps and revisions: some pieces, for example, peter out on a comma. Few texts here match the density and economy of the earlier published poems, and nothing can match the beauty of something like this:

> Wherever we turn in the storm of roses
> the night is lit with thorns, and the thunder
> of leaves, so quiet in the bushes,
> follows on our every step.

Yet, in their intensity and in their anguish, they are fascinating documents with flashes of inspired writing and a starkness which gives them a power of their own.

Although many of the poems lack the gesture of opening outwards towards the universal that lifts a poem out of the private realm, it would be wrong to think of these pieces simply as protocols of a soul in despair. As has been pointed out many times, the gesture of authenticity is always also an aesthetic gesture. And if one looks beyond the emotive subject matter, one sees the poetic consciousness at work – despite herself: 'without music, without defiance [. . .] not out of spite / but in spite of everything'. There is a limpidity and knowingness to some texts which is breathtaking: 'I wasn't even afraid of your hands / only sometimes and too late'; or 'It's dangerous to love, a crime / to impose.' The ends of the poems in particular are often finely balanced: a poem 'For Ingmar Bergman, who knows about the wall', for example, which refers back, as many of the pieces do, to Bachmann's cycle of novels, *Todesarten* [Ways of Dying], describes a series of horrifying hospital visions, but concludes coolly: 'madness, in which / everything, for all I care / everything, for all I care / can go under.' And they are filled with quotations: quotations from Hölderlin, Gaspara Stampa, *Tristan and Isolde*. Bachmann, the opera lover, in a long poem about hatred, suddenly cites Tosca springing heroically to her death, but in a later poem, when she again takes up the image of 'leaping from the uppermost terrace', it is far more subdued and grimly ironic: 'a dead body straight / after breakfast would have / spoiled your day'. There are more public poems too which bridge the personal and political in a characteristically slippery way: 'I doubt. But let it come, / the revolution. Also of my heart.' The 'better world' of the title is surely both an injunction for a more humane way of living and a better way of being in the world 'among brothers'.

The architecture of the collection as presented seems to suggest, after the long despair, a moment of redemption ('Night of Love') and a gradual reassertion of the self. It is impossible to say whether this is a true or hoped-for narrative, as the edition does not contain the scholarly apparatus, the formal dating and explanation of editorial principles which would allow one to make such assumptions. This was one of the aspects of the book which caused such vociferous criticism in Austria and in the German press. What is clear, however, is that these texts offer a uniquely revealing insight into Bachmann at her lowest ebb. They are more physical, more despairing, more unguarded and unfinished than anything published in her lifetime. In almost every sense they are unauthorised: bringing her closer than ever before, but also filled with profound doubts about the legitimacy of her own voice, her own authorship. For some they sell the best of her work short, and the very inadequacy of the volume further serves the mythologisation which has been such a damaging part of Bachmann's reputation. On the other hand, however, they are a fascinating insight into how a poem takes shape and emerges from the wreckage of really lived experience. Finally, they are sometimes luminous, sometimes oppressive, but memorable lines of poetry which deserve to reach a wider readership.

Torture

Said it
and the light
went out,
wrote it, and
someone fell to dust
an old dress

(The translations in this Introduction are by Karen Leeder. The first nine of the following poems are from the posthumous collection *Ich weiss keine bessere Welt*.)

Details of the volume: Ingeborg Bachmann, '*Ich weiß keine bessere Welt*', *Unveröffentliche Gedichte*, ed. by Heinz Bachmann, Isolde Moser and Christian Moser, München: Piper, 2000, 195 pp., ISBN 3-492-04255-4.

Farewell

We shall be the furthest, no greeting
will be returned any more, no word is still
worth employing. Also the microbe under
the glass, the guinea pig too on which
an experiment ends fatally and which,
twitching and poisoned, can no longer
cry out Good Lord, these are my comrades.
I look for all mistreated creatures,
those worn out and the thrown-away glass,
the discarded garments, the burnt-out houses that shriek
to heaven, and I make do with the residue.
All these are my kindred.
Brotherly love is practised on us, we are patched up,
instilled with trust and moved
to another place.

This place is good, here we are still
reachable only by death, a stupid guinea pig,
a squashed louse, a blissful heart,
reachable no longer by naked fear,
cloaked in the pauper's smock of brotherly love.

Goodbye

The flesh that has aged so well with me,
the parchment hand that kept mine cool,
let it lie on that whitened thigh,
let flesh grow young again, in an instant,
so that decay takes hold more swiftly.
The lines have come swiftly, everything above
the taut muscle frame already slightly sunken.

Not to be loved. The pain could be greater.
Lucky the one whose door slams shut.
But the flesh – with the fault line on the knee,
the wrinkled hands, all appearing overnight,
the weathered shoulder blade, where no green grows –
once it was shelter for a face.

Aged by a hundred years in a day.
The trusting beast, under the lash of the whip,
is robbed of pre-established harmony.

How difficult forgiving is . . .

How difficult forgiving is,
such a slow and gruelling task,
it's been my only occupation
for so many years.

Hatred has made me ill,
I'm disfigured, these pus-filled boils
forbid me to show myself
among my fellows.

I know only that I
cannot go on hating like this,
cannot wish for your death,
which I do not wish for at all
or by my hand.

I have learnt that I
must love my enemies, and
this is so easy, for how then
should my enemies
do me worse than evil?
If a bullet goes astray,
if someone spits in my face,
as yesterday, I have no misgivings
about the love prescribed for me.

I am afraid, of the love
you have instilled in me
with the cruellest intent.
Quite corroded by biting acids,
by all that arsenic, the opium,
quite numbed by my destruction.
Since I'm no longer alive in you
and am already dead where I am.
Counting the bars, enduring,
feeding myself twice a day,
then relieving myself,
begging for the means
to plunge me into sleep for a year.

Jewish Cemetery

Forest of stone, no special graves, nowhere to kneel
and nowhere for flowers. Each stone is so cramped there,
as if clinging to the other's neck, none unmindful of the
    other,
offering the living a hair's breadth to pass through
without grief. On reaching the exit, you have not death
but the day in your heart.

My Poems Have Gone Astray

My poems have gone astray.
I look for them in every corner of the room.
Don't know in my pain how to write
a pain, know nothing any more.

Know that one cannot just keep blathering on,
more spice is needed, a seasoned metaphor
should come to mind. But with the knife in my back.

Parlo e tacio, parlo. I escape into an idiom,
in which even some Spanish occurs, los toros y
los planetas, perhaps still to be heard
on some old stolen record. A bit of French
would also do, tu es mon amour depuis si longtemps.

Adieu, you lovely words, with all your promises.
Why have you abandoned me? Were you not well?
I have put you on deposit with a heart, one of stone.
Work for me there, keep at it there, do a thing for me there.

Night of Love

In a night of love after a long night
I have learnt to speak again and I wept
because a word came out of me. I have learnt to walk again,
walked up to the window and said hunger and light
and night was fine by me for light.

After an overlong night
slept peacefully again
trusting in this,

I spoke more easily in the dark,
spoke on through the day,
ran my fingers over my face,
I am no longer dead.
A bush, from which fire leapt in the night.
My avenger stepped out and called himself life.
I even said: let me die, and meant
without fear my kinder death.

Ingeborg Bachmann

Smells

I've always loved the smell, the sweat,
the morning effluvia, and the excrement,
the filth from a long rail-trip and in a bed.

My smell has been damned, I reeked
of liquor in a well-ordered house.
Three baths a day no rarity. At the month's end
I have been avoided like a corpse.

I have regretted much, but most of all my smell.
Most of all that my smell has not been liked.
That breeds hatred; vengefulness and damnation too are
   bred.

So we might die . . .

So we might die,
not to be parted;
your house must
remain my house.
I must go in and out,
must remain there,
see things are right,
since no one else sees
what your withered eyes
find at evening, just me,

I know, hence your house
must always
be my house
wherever I am. I must
see to the evening
and lift the thoughts
up into sleep.

Wooing

I woo everyone
and win no one –
the tram conductor
who snaps the door shut
in my face, the postman
who rings
too loudly – I woo
everyone, I need
a host of people
to be able to love them.
It's risky to love people,
a criminal act
to impose oneself.

The Game Is Over

Dearest brother, when shall we build a raft
and float across the sky and down?
Dearest brother, our overloaded craft
will founder soon and we shall drown.

Dearest brother, let's draw on paper fair
lots of lands and railway lines.
On those black lines look out, take care,
or you'll be blown up by the mines.

Dearest brother, I'm willing to be tied
screaming and yelling to the stake.
But you from death's dark vale already ride;
together our escape we'll make.

Alert in gypsy camp and desert tent,
we feel the sand run through our hair.
Your age and mine and the world's ages spent
can never be computed year by year.

Don't be fooled by the spider's sticky hand,
by sly ravens, by feathers in the bush.
Neither eat nor drink in Never Never Land,
illusion foams in every pan and dish.

He alone has won who on the bridge of gold
still knows the garnet fairy's code.
I must tell you that all this, like snows of old,
has melted, from the garden flowed.

From many, many stones our feet are sore.
One's sound. Let's skip then till the children's king,
the kingdom's key held gleaming in his jaw,
arrives to fetch us. Then we'll sing:

'Good times are coming when the date stone sprouts!
Each one that falls is on the wing.
Red foxglove makes the hem for paupers' shrouds,
your leaf bud rests on my signet ring.'

We must sleep now, dearest, the game's eclipsed.
We go on tiptoe. Nightshirts billow white.
Our parents say the house will be bewitched
if we exchange our breaths at night.

The translators gratefully acknowledge the helpful advice they had from Karen Leeder in their work on these poems. The editors acknowledge with thanks the permissions granted them by Heinz Bachmann and Isolde and Christian Moser.

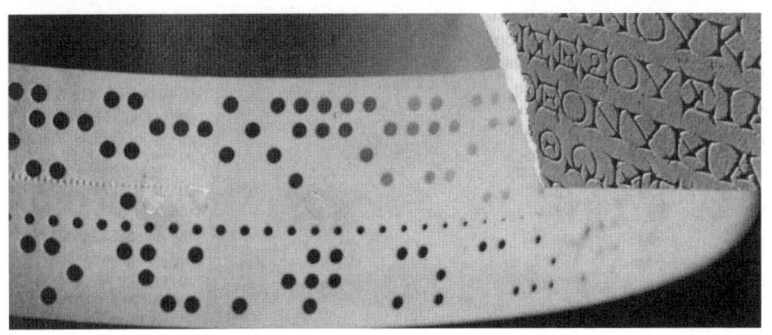

Rimbaud
Versions of Three Poems
by Martin Bennett

On the Road (Ma bohème)

Hands inside punctured pockets, I'd decamp,
Patched jacket to match the summer moon –
Stride scanning iamb, spondee, iamb –
The Muses' lackey, senses in a swoon.

My trousers had reached the point of no repair.
Fugitive Tom Thumb, with rhymes I'd strew
Each wayside. At the Inn of the Great Bear
The original All Stars plied their sweet frou-frou:

I tuned into it, a galactic France Inter.
To cool my brow there was dew's elixir.
Yet still the verses swarmed; nature or art –
Shadows now like Bacchae now like Graces,
As for want of a lyre I plucked the laces
Of my boots, one foot clasped against my heart.

Temptress (La Maline)

The dining room was brownly grandiose;
Fruit and varnish perfumed the air.
I was downing a plate of Belgian potatoes,
My body dwarfed by an enormous chair.

The clock sounded a minor symphony
On the hour. A rustle on the kitchen stair
And with a sly dishevelled hint at why,
The maidservant entered, mane of auburn hair

Tumbling about her shoulders, little finger
To her lips. She cleared the plates, then lingered
So close that my eyes couldn't help but stray:

How butterflies of desire fluttered and flew,
Her downy cheek touched by the sun's last ray,
Her décolletage a dream come true . . .

Vowels (Voyelles)

A: Are you a Hillbilly or an upside-down flower?
    On the tongue you are sweet vermouth,
    To the eye a wigwam initialling catatonic plains.
    To think you started as a fly escaping some ogre's mouth;
    Look how you have changed.

E: The bird is green. With jet-black eyes
   It peers out from a backdrop of sunburned yellow
   A continent of grass ago –
   O aerials, derricks, smokestacks,
   Or are you a Martian's hat perhaps,
   The tresses of Mimi?

I: 's the colour of railroad tracks,
   A robot's cryptic smile. Bold as a tree
   In whose branches a phone rings forever and a day.
   Striped with rain, it stands at attention,
   Cap an inky extra that sometimes disappears.

O: The mouth monocled, shape and essence of surprise itself,
   Where would we be without you?
   Exit and mysterious entrance, so large, so small,
   Porthole onto all our words cannot say.

U: Owl's favourite, this one conjures foghorns,
   A cavern's gape, sagacious beards –
   Brightly-scarfed skaters flashing across lakes in Finland –
   Turquoise twisting in the dark . . .

Bertolt Brecht
Ten Poems of Exile
Translated by Timothy Adès

Bertolt Brecht (1898–1956) is more widely known to English-speakers as a playwright than as a poet. In both genres, he is in the front rank. Poetry is more difficult to deliver and to receive, and also to translate; and Brecht himself gave more attention to presenting his plays. As a poet he mastered many styles. He drew on nursery songs, popular songs, jazz, Luther, *Des Knaben Wunderhorn*, Villon, Rimbaud, Kipling, the Japanese Noh theatre. His use of rhyme is especially powerful.

Brecht left Germany in 1933 and went to Denmark, then to Sweden and Finland: he was still there in 1941. He passed through the Soviet Union, and settled in Hollywood, returning in 1948 to East Berlin as a theatre director. All the poems offered here are from the Scandinavian period: later on, themes of exile probably faded from his mind.

Most of the following poems are not already collected in English, or at least not in the fine collection made with many translators by the late John Willett and Ralph Manheim. Their indispensable introduction brings out the central position of Brecht's poetry in his work, and the special reasons for its relative obscurity. The priority, for himself and others, had to be his plays.

Thanks are due to Suhrkamp Verlag, Mr Stefan S. Brecht and the Brecht Estate, and Methuen Ltd.

The Emigration of Poets

Homer was homeless: Dante
Had to leave his native city.
Li-Po and Tu-Fu wandered through civil wars
That devoured 30 million people
They threatened Euripides with the law
And they held the dying Shakespeare's mouth shut.
François Villon had not just the Muse
But the police after him.
Lucretius dubbed 'the Beloved'
Went into exile
So did Heine and so too
Brecht fled under the Danish thatch.

In the Second Year of my Exile

In the second year of my exile
I read in a newspaper, in a foreign language
That I had lost my nationality.
I was not sad and not joyful
When I read my name among many others
Good and bad.
Those who had fled seemed to me no more unfortunate
Than those who had stayed.

The Medea of Lodz

This is an old old story
Of a woman Medea by name
It was a thousand years ago
To a foreign land she came.
The man she loved had brought her
From far across the sea
And anywhere my home is
He said your home shall be.

She spoke another language
The people had not heard
For milk and bread and loving
They had another word.
Her hair was not like their hair
She walked with a difference
She never was accepted
They looked at her askance.

We know the fate she suffered
From old Euripides
Who sings in mighty chorus
Their trumped-up calumnies.
The wind blows over the rubble
Of that unfriendly town
Dust are the stones that stoned her
And struck the stranger down.

In our own time repeated
We hear that old refrain
They say that in our cities
Medeas are seen again.
Mid cars and trams and railways
The cry is heard once more
In our own city of Berlin
In 1934.

Exile

I
They take only what they need for subsistence
From their foreign surroundings. They are sparing
With their reminiscences.

No one gives them a call. No one pulls them back, or
    forward.
No one rebukes them and no one praises them.

As they have no present
They try to eke out time. Only to reach their goal
Which is a long way off
Do they try to better themselves.

Pre-occupied, they pick listlessly
At a bit of food. Sleepless,
They seek no lodging.

Their forebears
Are closer to them than their contemporaries
And seeming to have no present
They look with the greatest longing
To their successors.

What they say is said from memory
They move without passport or papers.

II
You are like people who reach the seashore
Want to cross and have only a spoon
To drain the sea. Or people
Who fall off a tower and ponder on the way down
How they might have built it higher.

As if you lived in a generous time. And that's the way of it.

III
They sawed off the branches they were sitting on
And yelled out that they had learnt
How to saw faster, and went
With a crack hurtling down, and those who watched them
Shook their heads as they sawed and
Went on sawing.

Homecoming of Odysseus

Look, that's the roof. The first concern is cleared.
Smoke from the house. There's somebody inside.
Even before they left the ship, they feared
All but the moon might be transmogrified.

On an Emigrant

Before him went the fame of his power, not of his
    achievement. Now
He follows. Powerless. He sits, stranded
On someone else's chair, a beginner
Who is already finished. His presumption
Comes from the past. Useful
He was. Dangerous
He is no longer, and surely won't be.
If he stays proudly at home, he hasn't the home to do it in.
If he comes back, he's looking for warmth. Ah, he has fools
Giving him advice now! Inferior specimens
Deny his talents. A master of language,
He must grope for words to say he's sorry. Even the silliest
    things
Must be learnt here, as never before. In his situation
It's time to know the value of learning.

Murderers drove him out, all right.
Butchers stayed behind.   *Fragment*

The Emigrant's Lament

Like you, I earned and ate my crust.
I am a doctor. No: I *was*.
By shade of hair and shape of nose
My roof and daily bread were lost.

I slept with one for seven year,
Hand on her belly, cheek on cheek.
She went to court about my hair:
Got rid of me. My hair was black.

I sought (at night through woods I fled:
By the wrong mother I was foaled)
A land where we were not accursed.

But if I asked to earn my bread,
Then shameless, shameless I was called.
I am not shameless: I am lost.

Legend of the Origin of the Book Lao-Te-Ching On Lao-Tse's Journey into Exile

He was seventy, unsteady
And the Teacher craved his rest
For in the land the good were all unready
And the bad were doing best.
So in boots and cloak he dressed.

So he packed to meet his need:
Bits and pieces, that was all,
Took the book he always read,
Good old pipe when shadows fall,
Roughly reckoned store of bread.

So he turns to cross the pass:
Last fond glance, the dales recede.
And his ox had fine fresh grass,
Lugged his master, chewed his feed.
Man's too old to care for speed.

On the fourth steep, stony day
A toll-gatherer barred his way.
'Valuables?' 'No. Nil to pay.'
'He's a teacher,' said the boy who led the beast.
So that much was clear, at least.

'Did he profit from that at all?'
Asked the fellow, in genial mood.
Said the boy, 'He learnt that durable
Stone yields in time to the waterfall:
By the soft the hard can be subdued.'

Not to waste the light, the boy
Drove the beast of burden on:
Round a black fir they were gone.
Suddenly something stirred the man.
'Stop!' he shouted. 'You there! Hoy!

'Old man! What's that about the water?'
Said the sage, 'Is that of use
To you?' Said he, 'I only gather
Tolls: but for tales of win-and-lose
I've time. If you know, please spill the news!

'Have the boy write it as you tell!
Such things mustn't be taken from us!
We have paper, ink as well,
Supper also. Look, my home is
Down there. Do we have a promise?'

The sage turned, looked at the fellow.
Coat of patches, had no shoe,
Forehead just a single furrow.
This was no victorious hero.
And he murmured, 'Even you?'

The old man would not, being old,
Turn down a polite request.
He said, 'One ought not to withhold
Answers.' Said the boy, 'It'll soon be cold.'
'Good: we'll halt and take a rest.'

And the Teacher clambered down
From his ox. Seven days they wrote as one.
The man brought food, and all the while
Swore at his smugglers in new style,
Softly. And the thing was done.

One day the customs-man receives
Eighty-one pithy sentences.
The sage thanks him for a gift, and leaves,
Rounding the fir, for the fastnesses.
Could there be greater courtesies?

But let's not only praise the sages
Whose names adorn our printed pages!
From the wise, wisdom must be wrested.
And so let's thank that man who levied charges:
He asked the question: he was interested.

Dance in Finland

Down by the pond at last night's dance
The exile made an appearance
To study the practices of the land
That gave him compassionate clearance.

Pigeon-Chest swung through the groaning throng
Clumsy was capering with him.
The first of the pair was gasping for air
The second was scrabbling for rhythm.

Old Bag and Young Bag were shaking a leg
Old Bag was the livelier mover.
Young Bag jumped round any holes in the ground
But Old Bag jumped right over.

Can you imagine! Two comrades-in-arms:
The blind man leading the maimed.
The blind said goodbye to his one glass eye
The cripple's good ankle was lamed!

The Master whirled the Housemaid along
In a devilish tight formation.
He stank of schnapps, their timing was wrong
She stank of perspiration.

Money and Justice were whooping it up
Long married, still deeply in love
They looked with surprise into each other's eyes
Which they noticed they just didn't have.

Patriotism and Patience combined
In a dance that was slowest of all.
I saw they were intimately entwined
Or else they'd have taken a fall.

Poverty with Stupidity hopped
I was almost reduced to tears.
Stupidity prattled and never stopped
Fraught Poverty lent him her ears.

Hunger was leading Work about
They were not unknown to each other.
They danced in step and they never got out
After years of marriage together.

A fiddle played and a clarinet
And a mouth-organ over the water
They all played the dancers a minuet
But it wasn't the same sonata.

The birch-trees all stood shuddering by
The new moon just couldn't take it
By the twentieth round his gorge rose high
He used the pond as a bucket.

Pantry in Finland 1940

Food in cool shade! The dark fir's smell comes blowing
In at your window when the day has gone.
Great pitcher of sweet milk appends its perfume,
And the smoked bacon on the chilly stone.
Goat's-cheese and beer and fresh-baked bread and berries
Plucked from grey shrubs at fall of morning dew!
All you whom war detains with empty bellies
Beyond the sea: might I play host to you!

Ivan Radoev
Three Poems
Translated by Kapka Kassabova

In one of his late poems, written shortly after the fall of the Berlin Wall and entitled 'A ballad written over there by a madman', Ivan Radoev writes:

> And now, let's fill in the form.
> Born – why?
> Education – pointless.
> Profession – enemy.

The 'madman' of the poem is the voice of the nation's alter-ego, finally free but immeasurably damaged by decades of totalitarian abuse. It was Radoev's speciality to speak about unspeakable things in ways which, albeit censored by eagle-eyed editors on the lookout for 'moral decadence', managed to see the light of print throughout his life. His poems, often called ballads and tales, are richly ironic, elliptical allegories of the absurdity and sorrow of life, both on a metaphysical and a political level. Born in small-town Bulgaria in 1927 and destined to live his most active creative life under communism,

Radoev is one of Bulgaria's most original and distinguished lyrical poets and playwrights. His exceptional sensibility and integrity as an artist who never took the easy Faustian path of pandering to power is matched by the extraordinary philosophical, aesthetic, moral and formal scope of his poetry, on a par with his far better-known Slavic contemporaries Zbigniew Herbert and Wislawa Zsymborska. The three poems offered here are a modest sample from an extremely rich body of work, yet to be revealed in its fullness to English-language readers.

Eclipse

Time built its shadow
into words, which then collapsed.
Who is banging at the gates for help?
Oh, that's eternity.

(Seconds are centuries – wrote the pulp fiction.
I have over-jumped myself three hundred times – wrote the flea.
I have not counted the drops – wrote the ocean.)

And I wrote myself a tree, put a bird in it,
made a table and a chair, and went away.

Welcome, make yourselves at home – I am no longer here.

Optimism

The obscure and the simple
go hand in hand.

A horse is grazing by the river –
how simple.

A child is asking: why?

Come, centuries and eras,
come Greeks, Egyptians, Persians, Thracians.
Come Aristotles and laureates, physicists
and natural philosophers,
sociologists and urbanists.
Bring your electronic brains!
Bring your formulas!

Here's the round table,
round like a zero.
Sit down.

A child is asking: why?
Now answer.

What a long pause of knowledge.

And now, let's rest.
A horse is grazing by the river . . .

Savagery

I'm for not staying.
For spitting out our last words –
for drinking vinegar instead of wine
and for the century to wash its hands.

I'm for it. Here's the abyss.
Let us take off our faces – without prayers,
with one quick movement, let us get engulfed.

I'm for this world final.
But let us leave our children on the hill.

Someone has to be there to curse us.

Any Ideas? Calling all Poetry Detectives

In the *MPT* New Series Number 13 (1998), I wrote a short review of the Irish poet Denis Devlin's *Translations into English* edited by Roger Little (Dedalus, 1992). I drew attention to the fact that the volume contains an appendix entitled 'Translations from Untraced Sources'. It crossed my mind that the collective knowledge of poetry translations possessed by readers of *MPT* might enable the authors of some of these extracts to be identified. It turned out that there was not room in that issue to reprint the appendix. However, when I mentioned the unfinished business to the new editors of *MPT*, they readily agreed to reprint it now in the hope that readers would enjoy the not so trivial pursuit of identifying these eleven poems or fragments of poems. Any successes will be acknowledged in *MPT* and forwarded to Roger Little.

Anthony Rudolf

Untitled

The gentle fortune of death soon smoothing
I would not let him say
With that voice shrouded in stone
That I'd loose [*sic*] nothing by being plastered on the back of
  a ditch
Although I could manage fine to live with alluvial earth
Whose suddenly flashing waterdrops would glisten in
  mockery
Over my body hiding from the mainstreet of the sun.
Like mocking laughter at night down an alley
Dishonour therefore to the courtiers of space
Their — words may they swallow hard not that
The laughter thirsty king that has them well in hand
Would take from them the shivering top of their compass.
All the same, look out; the sooner the blarney of your
  mouths is ensoiled
The sooner I'll be changed into perfume
On account of my dependence on the stuff of inflammable
  lips
Nothing in my little rushes bench, is in my heart
Is worth competing with lascivious sick refuse
Windbag boaster breasted, whose cry was suffocated back.

South Wall

The north cone has been flying this last couple of days
    and more
The local watermen
Stare at pilings in the mud.

Untitled

Let them not think of themselves thinking, as if the die
Mattered or could see itself when the stamp
Is unknown, unloved so
Let not misuse of instruments make them mad.
Such men exist, find them, and bring me to them.

II
The sun on the green iron post
The sun on the stela with the national hero
The sun on the obelisk
On the green lawn, the sun
O Aengus Dei [*sic*]

When I was in my room above
And looks [*sic*] out the window on the town
I saw the riff-raff and the splendid girls
Oily and seductive with wide arms
The sun all over the wide sea
            Vos, clarissima mundi
Lumina.

Untitled

The front garden, small athletic shrubs
I passed through and entered the soft room
And felt the carpet saw the instruments
The brother of my lady was to play
And worried, being past student age,
That taxi drivers quarrel when they are rich
That the dog was put in the bathroom with the bitch.

Untitled

The footballer divests himself in speechless promotion
The mature superintendent steps out of her panties.
The train's margin of safety is the buffers
As it slows down with a satisfied chuckling of all its
   couplings.

Untitled

Beneath the lifeless banners of the sky
Of gray light the sun could not pierce through
As if they had shuddered in death throes and lay
Still, the packed disinterested clay
Spread for miles with none to do it proud
A herd of horses drifted like a cloud

Untitled

They could not pass by the southern seas
Bordered by pomegranates and owned by peoples
Whose legend played through silk and gods of the lyre
They turned therefore to what seemed forbidden
The thousand mile ice gummed north.

Nel Fra Tempo: Abschied

Shut the eyes and let the mineral dark
Shine and immerse me in a starry sleep
Then sweetness breaks smoothly like
Snow on the cheeks and shoulders; in that vast
Worldless and impecunious horror.

Les Carolines

Coy precision in her care of the sick
And of her uniform is a mercy to the nurse
With this rosary she mesmerises her fear
Born of an ugly face
Meanwhile her story of the hobo
And his brother the policeman who followed him into
 Western Union
To find the hobo is remembered

Untitled

No tulip petals waver more discreet about the rain frittered
   gods in Versailles
Whose broad mellow sun curtains that avenue
The next stop infinity

La Grande Nation

> *Men are we and must weep when even the shade*
> *Of that which once was great has passed away.*
>   Wordsworth

The Colonel, the army is the enemy
To me, sick neutral clerk no longer enemy
For the sadness in his eyes about his son
And my wife's friends from the Alpine University
Faithful brown eyes, piercing wrists
All snow flashing and bred with blood

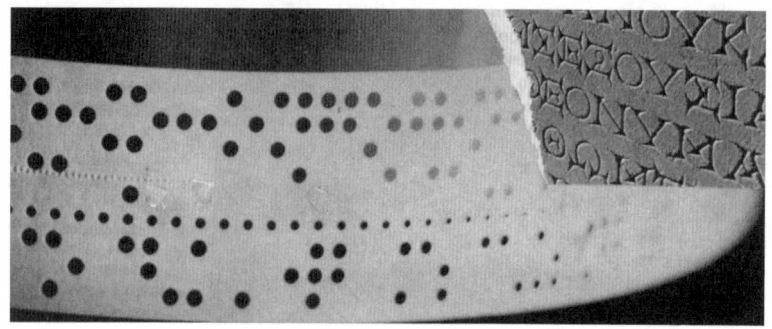

Josephine Balmer
A Note on Reviewing Translation

What are we doing when we review a translation? Are we judging the original source text? Or its translated version? Or perhaps the methodology used by the translator? And how are we qualified to speak, let alone to judge? Unfortunately many reviewers in the mainstream literary pages seem quite happy to side-step such issues, treating a translation as if it were the original, often barely noticing the presence of the translator, let alone acknowledging it. Even when a translation is accredited, reviews can still be inadequate; reviewers who have almost certainly never come across a word of Urdu or Polish or Flemish – and probably wouldn't know it if they did – nevertheless feel quite free to pronounce a translation 'jarring' or to pounce on a single word as 'infelicitous'. Then there are those with some knowledge of the source language but no real experience of literary translation beyond a prejudice that it is an impossible task and therefore almost always a failure.

But reviews written within the translation world can sometimes be as problematic as those from without. Often there is the same confusion about what the task in hand might represent. Those with a profound knowledge of the original can be tempted to spend their allotted word allowance on a discussion of its merits or shortcomings at the expense of the translation's own qualities. Then there is the methodology of the review itself. Some reviewers, for instance, adopt a soap-box approach, seizing the opportunity to champion or chastise a particular school of translation theory – faithful versus free, perhaps – with the work at hand often in danger of becoming a casualty of the crossfire.

Similarly, a comparative approach is common, examining other, different versions alongside the translation at hand – a useful tool, no doubt. Yet without due care, this can sometimes degenerate into a critical beauty pageant, lining up several variants of a few lines or even a few words like competing contestants, as if somewhere in the ether, a definitive, monolithic version awaits discovery (less modest reviewers even put forward their own as answer) and once found the search is over. Yet, as the model of classical translation teaches, what seems right in one precise moment in time might not necessarily seem right in the next; over the centuries what becomes important is not how much better – or worse – one translation conveys the original than any other, but what it teaches about the circumstances of that text's transmission, its afterlife (for how is it ever possible to decide between, say, Jonson or Dryden?).

This begs a further question: do you need to know the original source language in order to review a translation? Clearly a linguist's eye can alert the reader to the nuances of the text, discussing the various ways in which the translator has approached them. And yet, while obviously a welcome approach, this emphasis on the linguistic can occasionally be at the expense of the literary; of an understanding and sympathy of the translation per se, as a new piece of literature in its target culture. After all, translations are written primarily for those with no access to the source language and amongst all the detailed discussions of altered word order or slight variation of line length, it is important to remember this. Sometimes an intuitive, informed reader with a good working knowledge of the field, if not the branch, can see the bigger picture more clearly than those overwhelmed by the minutiae.

Nevertheless, there are, of course, many talented critical writers in our profession, a good deal of whom regularly write for this journal. So what should we expect from a translation review? My aim in these pages is to publish reviews which chime with the ethos of this new series of the journal: to be all encompassing, all embracing. To be incisive and critical, of course, but also compassionate. For this we need first of all an understanding of the process of translation, of the many paths that may or may not be taken along that hard road from original to version, all different, all equal. An understanding that translation, like all literary endeavours, revolves around the act of choice – and that such choices are not necessarily compromises, as often assumed, but informed judgements, both technical and creative, made after careful consideration. An awareness that the choices we make today might not necessarily be the same as those we make tomorrow; that a version might always be different, other. Add to that a creative, intelligent and above all sympathetic appreciation of the translator's art. For translation is about courage; about facing up to the impossibility of a task and yet still finding ways to accomplish it, of somehow squaring the circle. Above all, though, reviewers need to be able to write. Good reviews tell us not only something of the book – will I like it? do I want to buy it? – but also increase our understanding of art, and therefore of life.

Reviews

Claire Malroux
Birds and Bison: Poems
translated by Marilyn Hacker
The Sheep Meadow Press
New York 2004
ISBN 1-931-357-10-2
169pp. paperback £ 6.74 $ 12.95

Translating Echoes

In translating there is always the danger of translating too much or too little; at times the subtle graduations of one language have no equivalent and every individual voice worthy of the name has an ephemeral quality that can all too easily slip trough the translating process. What is awkward and grating in one language (and one must always assume that the effect is desired) can sound banal once it is translated into another. The gravest danger is always that a translator will inadvertently turn editor, smoothing out rough edges, giving an unobstructed flow to a text that relies on a contorting and twisting syntax.

In translating Claire Malroux's poems Marilyn Hacker has avoided some major pitfalls but there remains a disparity between the original text and the translation on the facing page. The words themselves match well enough, but what might irritate a French ear in the original has no equivalent in the English translation.

In one sense what matters is not the aesthetic quality of the original poetry but the accuracy of the translation; bad poetry that reaches greatness through the translation process is a bad translation (although it can be seen as an original in its own right, or, to borrow a term in its strict musical sense, it remains a great rendition). For this point not to appear as merely pedantic a brief digression is in order. Taking the example of photography we might say that as a medium it belongs to two worlds: photography as a visual art form, and as a vehicle for recording or documenting. Taking a photograph of a wart-infested face with a soft focus lens might result in a portrait of intrinsic aesthetic value, but in terms of documentation it will be misleading. In the same way that photography can fuse both roles when handled with mastery, translating poetry requires the re-creation of a work from one language into another. For it to be called a masterful translation it must fulfil its role as an accurate representation of the original before any aesthetic judgements can be levelled at it.

The poetry of Claire Malroux has an unusual twist insofar as it is inspired by her translations of the poetry of Emily Dickinson and Derek Walcott among others. Unlike many continental poets who turn to translation as a means to support themselves, her career has evolved in the opposite direction, indeed she is perhaps better known in France as a translator than as a poet. Aware of the danger that it would be all too easy to fall into imitating the poets she translates, what Malroux brings to her poetry in French is a cadence and syntax that 'disturbs' a native ear. Granted the twist is an ephemeral one; furthermore, the rapid shifts of images and avoidance of metaphorical unity or cohesiveness easily overshadow it. Nevertheless one can hear the echoes, it is as if Malroux were speaking French with a slight but purposeful American accent, the phrasing causes one to halt and turn back; to retrace the thought. These opening lines, for example, play on the reversal of verb and noun:

> Que la nature affirme une changeante identité
> Nous rassure. Le temps s'enroule sur le fuseau . . .

The reversal of the customary *une identité changeante* sounds like a tongue-in-cheek imitation of the English spoken in *Asterix*, but the next line re-establishes syntactical if not grammatical correctness. The translation reads 'That Nature affirms its mutability / Reassures us. Time rolls itself up onto the spindle . . .' The easy flow requires no work on the part of the reader and the statement edges towards a platitude.

The ease with which Malroux's lines can be kept in translation to a single line should have alerted Hacker that something was happening. Without the presence of that syntactical twist and its ephemeral impact, the translated poetry falls into belatedness or the overbearing shadow of debt. What would turn the present translation into a masterful one would be to hear the echo of a French accent *doing* an American accent.

Notwithstanding Marilyn Hacker's idiosyncratic note at the end of her introduction, the addition of titles to many of the translated poems is wholly unwarranted. If they were 'primarily to facilitate their submission to and publication in American and British literary magazines', now – in the book – was the opportunity to remove them. Titles such as 'Erosion', 'Hoarding', and 'Monument' add nothing to the poems and if anything pre-empt the reader's discovery of the topic by their generic pigeonhole nature.

However, if one translation can redeem this bilingual collection it is the second poem in the sequence 'Horizon Line':

Don't say black
black is a visionary color
intense and desiring substance
a diamond facet
attracting toward the density
of its depth

Cite blind transparency instead
the snare of emptiness

The hole would be a white-walled cube
a mirrored sphere
where a shadow twists
in search of a drop of blood
on the clouds' reflections

Olivier Burckhardt

Ileana Mălăncioiu
After the Raising of Lazarus
translated by Eiléan Ní Chuilleanáin
Southword Books
ISBN 1905002041
pb £8.99

Song of Joy

Translating contemporary poetry from countries which have strong lyrical and folk traditions is extremely hard. Whilst the translator wishes to preserve the lyrical nature of the poem, the same structures and traditions are not open to her in English. Somehow a freer verse structure must be found, with the appearance, rather than the presence of the often strictly metred and rhymed original form and melody must be suggested, rather than hammered out. Folk images require a delicacy of touch in English to avoid sentimentality and the combination of mythical and fairytale with contemporary can seem awkward and quixotic in contemporary English.

Often the demands on the translator prove too much and the whole endeavour fails – but not in this case. Ileana Mălăncioiu has found a translator equal to her poetry in Eiléan Ní Chuilleanáin. The translator opts with experience and wisdom for the simplest, clearest words and an intuitive melodic structure. She rarely reproduces the rhyme patterns of the original, but often hints at a rhyme or a binding structure. This creates the impression of a piece of tracing paper through which the original can be felt and even partly seen, and an honesty about the enterprise of translation. Many of the poems, in their spareness, achieve that rare thing: they become new poems in a strange poetic language, which is neither English, nor Romanian:

> It was a night almost sleepless, Lord, what a night it was
> And how afraid I was alone with Ieronim
> And his body shone so brightly that
> Through it appeared every one of his broken bones.

(From 'A Night Almost Sleepless')

The collection opens with a poem 'The Headless Bird' in which the poet takes the body of a slaughtered bird in one hand and the head in another. The head dies first and the poet feels death 'passing through' her to reach the body, like an electric current. This peculiar and powerful image, at once flesh and earth, and yet metaphor for the poet as a living conduit for death, sets the tone for this collection. Mălăncioiu's preoccupation with death, the rituals and event of it, is constant –

death is in us, around us, preparing to claim us. In the title poem 'After the Raising of Lazarus' the poet asks 'For how much time, for whom and for what / Did you raise me up?' Death is found in elements and objects, everyday *memento mori*, and Death is also a protagonist: in 'In my Steaming Mirror' Death washes her hair and combs it, and the mirror is where she waits for the fearful lyrical persona.

It is as if Mălăncioiu carries constantly inside her the sense of disbelief and wrongness which one feels after another's premature death. She circles around the theme of death asking over and over how it can be so, finding inexhaustible numbers of metaphors and images for life passing into death. And yet at the same time she has armed herself: the act of imagining and writing are the weapon and the shield against the fear of death. 'Forgive us this day our daily fear,' Mălăncioiu writes in a poem about the death of a son, 'Forgive us our fear'. In a desolating poem about visiting her sister who is dying, a horse appears to her – their own horse which died the year before, and it is outlined as if 'picked out in gold'. The dying woman gazes after it and the poet wonders again how it can be possible that there isn't a cure. How can it be possible, when life is so full of symbolism and miracle and human inner life is so rich?

Throughout Mălăncioiu's poetry vitality and death are placed alongside each other and the reader wonders with her at the random and incredible way in which death and life switch places. Indeed, in the poems which appear to be dedicated to her dead sister, death shifts between them. 'Your hair had grown' is a confusing tangle: a grandmother, 'you' and 'I' attempt to plait the hair, as if dressing a body – but the hair, symbol of strength and vitality, continues to grow. In 'Laid Beside You' the bodies themselves are interchangeable:

nobody knew I was buried,
if they had called to me I would have answered
from under the flat stone

which I had pulled slowly over me
without realising it
as I would draw a rug
where we were sleeping together
leaving you half bare.

(From 'Laid Beside You')

A revision of the Antigone myth shuffles both protagonists and elements, so that it is the 'traitor snow' which starving dogs come to tear at, and the hill to which she gives burial. The myth is jarred and bruised – Antigone mourns the landscape, and yet is buried alive in the hill which she has mourned like a sister. In this poem, as in others, it is hard not to see a political edge to Mălăncioiu's writing. The poem directly accuses the community of letting Antigone enter the tomb to die. Mălăncioiu herself was censored under Communist rule, and did not avoid politics in her poetry. On the evidence of this collection the political is mainly congruous with her poetics, an extension of her vision. Only the poem 'Monument' in which they are all working in chain-gangs to complete an enormous monument to the dead seems more overtly and completely political. Ní Chuilleanáin has reflected this in her choice of strict end rhymes for the translation.

'Song of Joy' makes the life equation plain. In this poem 'joy for all my life' coexists with 'one intense grief' – aging and death. In this delicate and extraordinary poem the rejoicing is remembered – even as it coincided with the passing:

There you brought me secretly sparrows' eggs
for my meal in the morning
and cuckoo's milk in the evening
and joy for all my life

and one intense grief
because it could not last
until old age.

After the Raising of Lazarus is a handpicked collection – Mălăncioiu's poetry has been published in Romanian for over forty years and so this can at best be a tiny part of her output. There is a sense that the translator has been able to choose those poems she feels *will* translate. As a result Mălăncioiu is represented at the height of her powers, by a translator at the height of her powers. There is barely a poem in it which does not offer revelation in its imagery, the strangeness of its voice or its perspective.

There is much to praise in this collection. Mălăncioiu is not afraid of rich multi-layered imagery, prophetic and political statement. Nor is she afraid of religious belief, which she wears in the poems without self-consciousness, in a robustly Old Testament spirit. Her poetry is dense with symbolism. Even in the contrasting spareness of her language she has an assurance and majesty.

Her poetry should be read for many reasons, not least because these translations offer English language poetry new strategies and ways of existing. We have rather cut ourselves off from poetry like Mălăncioiu's, which permits the presence of the grand and mythical, and in which there is a solemn and sincere belief in the continuity of imagination.

Sasha Dugdale

Shorter Reviews & Further Books Received

Bashô, *Bashô's Journey: The Literary Prose of Matsuo Bashô*, translated with an introduction by David Landis Barnhill, Suny, $17.95, ISBN 0-7914-6414-8

A companion volume to Barnhill's *Bashô's Haiku*, together forming an indispensable guide to this master of classical Japanese literature.

Moisés Castillo-Florián, *Reflecting on Reflections and Other Poems*, translated by the author with Alison Dent, Anaconda Editions, ISBN 1-901990-02-8

Castillo-Florián is a Peruvian poet now living in London and this interesting new volume, co-translated with Alison Dent, presents his linguistically sparse but thematically dense work in both English and Spanish, to be read, as the poet suggests, 'as a music score'.

Gerda Mayer, *Prague Winter*, Hearing Eye, £8.95, ISBN 1-870841-12-3

A poet's beautiful prose memoir of early childhood in Nazi-occupied Czechoslovakia

Knut Ødegård, *Judas Iscariot and Other Poems*, translated by Brian McNeill, Waxwing, £7.95, ISBN 0-9549771-0-6

New poems by the leading Norwegian poet, featured in *MPT* 3.2, available in English for the first time in Brian McNeill's highly readable translations

Madeleine Marie Slavick, *Delicate Access*, translations into Chinese by Luo Hui, Sixth Finger Press, ISBN 988-97075-2-7

A fascinating project from the Hong Kong-based Sixth Finger Press, Slavick's delicate English lyrics are here presented in a dual text edition with Chinese translations by Luo Hui.

Kristin Dimitrova, *A Visit to the Clockmaker*, translated from the Bulgarian by Gregory O'Donoghue, Southword Editions, £8, 1-905002-03-3;

Zbynek Hejda, *A Stay in a Sanatorium*, translated from the Czech by Bernard O'Donoghue, Southword Editions, £8, ISBN 1-905002-05-X;

Barbara Korun, *Songs of Earth and Light*, translated from the Slovene by Theo Dorgan, Southword Editions, £8, ISBN 1-905002-06-8;

Immanuel Mifsud, *Confidential Reports*, translated from the Maltese by Maurice Riordan, Southword Editions, £8, ISBN 1-905002-08-4;

Sigitas Parulskis, *The Towers Turn Red*, translated from the Lithuanian by Liz O'Donoghue, Southword Editions, £8, ISBN 1-905002-07-6

Five more new volumes from Cork's Southword Editions, which partner leading Irish poets with those from across Europe. The editions are beautifully produced and their role in bringing poetry from less well-known languages such as Maltese or Lithuanian to wider recognition is admirable. Highly recommended.

Books for review should be sent to Josephine Balmer, Reviews Editor, Modern Poetry in Translation, East Meon, St John's Road, Crowborough, East Sussex, TN6 1RW.

Notes on Contributors

Timothy Adès has won the John Dryden and Premio Valle-Inclán prizes, and two BCLA/BCLT awards, all for poetry translation, working mostly with rhyme and metre. His two books, Victor Hugo's *How to be a Grandfather* and Jean Cassou's *33 Sonnets of the Resistance and Other Poems*, appeared in 2002. His Classic Gallic Lipograms (Hugo's *Boaz* and five symbolist sonnets) appeared in *MPT* 8, and Louise Labé's *Elegies* in *MPT* 16. A substantial volume of Robert Desnos' poetry is in progress.

Radwa Ashour is an Egyptian novelist, critic and academic. She is professor of English at Ain Shams University, Cairo. She is the author of seven novels, three collections of short stories and four books of criticism books.

Josephine Balmer's recent books include *Chasing Catullus: Poems, Translations and Transgressions* and *Catullus:Poems of Love and Hate* (both Bloodaxe, 2004). She is currently chair of the Translators' Association and also Reviews Editor of *Modern Poetry in Translation.*

Mourid Barghouti is a poet born 1944 in Ramallah. He has published fourteen books of poetry. His *Collected Works* were published in one volume (1997). He has read his poetry in most of the Arab countries and in many European capitals. He was awarded the Palestine Award for Poetry (2000) and the Naguib Mahfouz Medal for Literature for his memoir *I Saw Ramallah* translated into many languages including English (by Ahdaf Soueif) and published in Britain by Bloomsbury, with an introduction by Edward Said. He has participated in many international poetry festivals including Poetry International and Aldeburgh Poetry Festival and Edinburgh Book Festival. He now lives in Cairo with his wife, the Egyptian novelist Radwa Ashour and their only son Tamim.

Helen Beer teaches Yiddish at University College London. She is working at a biography of Itsik Manger.

Martin Bennett lives in Rome where he is a teacher and part-time proof-reader at the University of Tor Vergata. His translations from Apollinaire, Pavese, Pasolini and others have appeared in previous issues of *MPT*.

Olivier Burckhardt, poet, essayist, and translator, is currently working on *Pencilled Lines on Poetry*, a book of essays on East/West poetics.

Amarjit Chandan has published six collections of poetry and two books of essays in Punjabi and one in English *Being Here* (The Many Press, 1993, 1995, 2005). His work has appeared in *MPT, Poetry Review, Critical Quarterly, Wasafiri, Index on Censorship, Papirus* (Turkey), *Erismus, Ombrela, Odos Panos* (Greece) and *Lettre Internationale* (Romania). He was amongst British poets on Radio 4 selected by Andrew Motion on National Poetry Day in 2001 and participated in the 13th International Aldeburgh Poetry Festival the same year.

Polly Clark: author of *Kiss,* and of *Take Me With You*, shortlisted for the 2005 TS Eliot Prize and Poetry Book Society Choice.

Mary-Ann Constantine is a research fellow at the University of Wales. She has published short stories in *Planet* and the the *New Welsh Review*.

Patrick Drysdale read English at Oxford and taught English and Introductory Linguistics at the Memorial University of Newfoundland. He subsequently worked as a lexicographer and editor of English language and literature textbooks for a Toronto publisher. He returned to England in 1982, runs a small estate, and writes poetry.

Sasha Dugdale is a consultant and translator for the Royal Court Theatre. Her first collection *Notebook* was published by Carcanet/Oxford Poets in 2003; her second is due out in 2007. Her translations of Tatiana Shcherbina, *Life Without: Selected Poetry and Prose*, were published by Bloodaxe in 2004.

Antony Dunn: Author of three poetry collections, most recently *Flying Fish*. He won an Eric Gregory Award in 2000.

Michael Hamburger's *Collected Poems* were published in 1995. His *Poems of Paul Celan* came out in 1988 and the fourth edition of his *Friedrich Hölderlin, Poems and Fragments* in 2004.

Kurdish poet **Choman Hardi** was born in the Middle East and came to the UK as a refugee in 1993. She wrote in Kurdish until five years ago when she gradually switched to English. Her first collection of poetry in English, *Life For Us*, was published by Bloodaxe in 2004. She has been educated in Oxford, London and Canterbury.

W.N. Herbert: well-known poet in Scots and English. His collections have been shortlisted for the Forward Prize, Saltire Prize, TS Eliot Prize and McVities Prize.

Kapka Kassabova was born in Bulgaria 31 years ago, moved to New Zealand in her teens, and currently lives in Edinburgh. Her UK poetry debut is *Someone Else's Life* (Bloodaxe, 2003). Her first novel *Reconnaissance* won the 2000 Commonwealth Writers' Prize for best first novel, Asia-Pacific. In 2002 she held the Creative NZ Berlin Writers' Residence. She was twice the NZ Cathay Pacific travel writer of the year, and her current project is a travel memoir.

Karen Leeder is Reader in German at the University of Oxford, and Fellow and Tutor in German at New College, Oxford. She has published widely on modern German literature, especially poetry, and has translated work by a number of German writers including Bertolt Brecht, Brigitte Oleschinski, André Kubiczek, and Thomas Kling. Recent publications include Michael Krüger *Scenes from the Life of a Best-selling Author*, (London: Harvill Press, 2002; pbk. Vintage 2004) and Raoul Schrott, *The Desert of Lop* (London: Macmillan Picador, 2004). Her translations of Evelyn Schlag's *Selected Poems* (Carcanet, 2004) won the Schlegel-Tieck Prize 2005. She is currently working on an anthology of poems *After Brecht* for Carcanet Press to be published in 2006.

Mike Lyons served in Army Intelligence in post-war Austria, then studied German at Edinburgh University. As a teacher, he became a Head of Modern Languages, subsequently teaching at Oxford Brookes University and Ruskin College. Felix Mitterer's verse monologue *Siberien* had its UK premiere in a translation by him and Patrick Drysdale.

Jamie McKendrick's last book of poems was *Ink Stone* (Faber, 2003). He edited the *Faber Book of 20th-Century Italian Poems* (2004) and is currently working on a translation of Giorgio Bassani's *The Garden of the Finzi-Contini*.

Hubert Moore works as a volunteer with the Write-to-Life project at the Medical Foundation for the Care of Victims of Torture. His most recent collection of poetry is *Touching down in Utopia* (Shoestring Press, 2002). His pamphlet *Beautifully kept things* was a winner in the 2003 Poetry Business Competition.

Pascale Petit: her most recent collection is *The Huntress* (2005), shortlisted for the T. S. Eliot Prize. She was selected in 2004 as one of the Next Generation poets.

MODERN POETRY IN TRANSLATION   Series 3   Number 1

INTRODUCTIONS

Edited by David and Helen Constantine
Cover by Chris Hyde

Contents

Editorial   David and Helen Constantine

Mahmoud Darwish *A State of Siege*, translated by Sarah Maguire and Sabry Hafez

Boris Ryzhy, nine poems, translated by Sasha Dugdale

Giorgio Caproni, *Ligurian Suite*, translated by Robert Hahn

Liam Ó Muirthile, five poems, translated by Bernard O'Donoghue

Eunice Odio, 'Ode to the Hudson', translated by Keith Ekiss and Mauricio Espinoza

Luciano Erba, eleven poems, translated by Peter Robinson

Philippe Jaccottet, from *Green Notebook*, translated by Helen and David Constantine

Jorge Yglesias, Two short essays and five poems, translated by Peter Bush

Gerhard Falkner, seven poems, translated by Richard Dove

'The Traveller' – *A Tribute to Michael Hamburger*, by Charlie Louth

Price £11
Available from www.mptmagazine.com

MODERN POETRY IN TRANSLATION   Series 3   Number 2

DIASPORA

Edited by David and Helen Constantine
Cover by Lucy Wilkinson

Contents
Editorial   David and Helen Constantine

Carmen Bugan, an essay and two poems
Yannis Ritsos, fifteen *Tristichs,* translated by David Harsent
David Harsent, three poems from *Legion*
Goran Simic, an essay and four prose poems
Forough Farrokhzad, four poems, translated by Gholamreza Sami Gorgan Roodi
Marzanna Bogumila Kielar, six poems, translated by Elzbieta Wójcik-Leese
Lyubomor Nikolov, six poems, introduced by Clive Wilmer, translated Miroslav Nikolov
Adel Guémar, four poems, translated by Tom Cheesman and John Goodby
A note on Hafan Books by Tom Cheesman
Sándor Márai, 'Funeral Oration', translated by George Gömöri and Clive Wilmer
Paul Batchelor, versions of Ovid's *Tristia*
Olivia McCannon, three poems
Yvonne Green, three poems
Ziba Karbassi, three poems, translated by Stephen Watts
Volker Braun, nine poems, translated by David Constantine
Wulf Kirsten, ten poems, translated by Stefan Tobler
Knut Ødegaard 'Taking out the Hives' translated by Kenneth Steven
Eugenio Montale, three uncollected poems, translated by Simon Carnell and Erica Segre

Reviews
Bernard Adams on George Szirtes's Agnes Nemes Nagy
Paschalis Nicolaou on David Connolly's Yannis Kondos
Will Stone on Antony Hasler's Georg Heym

Price £11
Available from www.mptmagazine.com

MODERN POETRY IN TRANSLATION   Series 3   Number 3

METAMORPHOSES

Edited by David and Helen Constantine
Cover by Lucy Wilkinson

Contents
Editorial   David and Helen Constantine

Akhmatova on the South Bank
Ruth Borthwick: Anna of all the Russias: Translating Akhmatova
Elaine Feinstein: An Evening for Akhmatova
Colette Bryce: Six poems
Sasha Dugdale: Five poems
Jo Shapcott: Five poems
George Szirtes (with Veronika Krasnova): Six poems
Marilyn Hacker: 'For Anna Akhmatova'

John Greening: 'Coming Soon. *Remastered from the Old Norse*'
Neil Philip: 'Twenty-one glosses on poems from *The Greek Anthology*'
Paul Howard: Versions of four sonnets by Giuseppe Belli
Terence Dooley: A version of Raymond Queneau's 'La Pendule'
Kathleen Jamie: Hölderlin into Scots. Two poems
Josephine Balmer: *The Word for Sorrow:* a work begins its progress

Ingeborg Bachmann
Karen Leeder: Introduction
Mike Lyons: 'War Diary'
Patrick Drysdale and Mike Lyons: Five poems

Sean O'Brien: A version of Canto V of Dante's *Inferno*
Cristina Viti: Eros Alesi's *Fragments*
Sarah Lawson and Malgorzata Koraszweska: Six poems by Anna Kühn-Cichocka
Marilyn Hacker: Guy Goffette's 'Construction-Site of the Elegy'
Belinda Cooke and Richard McCane: Six poems by Boris Poplavsky
Cecilia Rossi: Poems from Alejandra Pizarnik's *Works and Nights*
Terence Cave: A memorial note on Edith McMorran and a translation of Aragon's 'C'
Paul Batchelor: An essay on Barry MacSweeney's Apollinaire

Reviews
Antony Wood on Angela Livingstone's *Poems from Chevengur*
Josephine Balmer on Cliff Ashcroft's *Dreaming of Still Water* and Peter Boyle's Eugenio Montejo
Paschalis Nikolaou on Philip Ramp's Karouzos
Francis Jones on Jan Twardowski (translated by Sarah Lawson and Malgorzata Koraszweska) and *A Fine Line: New Poetry from Central and Eastern Europe*

Price £11
Available from www.mptmagazine.com

Wasafiri

Issue no 47 Spring 2006

Interviews Chimamanda Ngozi Adichie and Helen Oyeyemi; Nayantara Sahgal **Articles** Alexander McCall Smith's Mma Ramotswe Novels; Indian Nationalism in Raja Rao's Short Stories; Prefaces to Colonial Modernist Texts; Salman Rushdie's *The Ground Beneath Her Feet* **Art** Contemporary Art Criticism and African Cultural Production **Poetry** Diana Bridge, John Haynes, Lou Smith **Fiction** Sampurna Chattarji *The Saint Who Resurrected a Goat*; Erica Johnson Debeljak *She's a Little Bit Unsure About the Formation of Clouds*; Victor Ehikhamenor *Who Will Bury the Dead?* **Reviews** Leila Aboulela *Minaret*; Caryl Phillips *A Distant Shore* & *Dancing in the Dark*; Salman Rushdie *Shalimar the Clown*; Walter Mosley *The Man in My Basement* & *A Red Death*; Bashabi Fraser *Tartan & Turban*; N D Williams *Julie Mango*; Smita Agarwal *Wish-granting Words*; Cornelia Sorabji *India Calling*; Kwame Anthony Appiah *The Ethics of Identity*

Summer 2006, no 48 Special Issue on Life Writing
Including: **Anthony Carrigan** *Personal Identity and Cultural Memory in Olaudah Equiano* **Anne Collett** *Jamaica Kincaid's Garden* **Chiji Akoma** *Ink* **Bart Moore Gilbert** *Western Autobiography and Colonial Discourse* **Blake Morrison**, **Hanif Kureishi** and **Susheila Nasta** *in Conversation* **Caryl Phillips** *Border Crossings*; **Tobias Döring** *Edward Said and the Fiction of Autobiography* Plus **Aamer Hussein, Jackie Kay, Jamaica Kincaid, Jane Bryce**

Winter 2006, no 49 Special Issue on Queer Writing
Including: **Chris Dunton, Jarrod Hayes** *Memmi's Queer Zionism*, **Suniti Namjoshi** *Poems and fables* Interview: **Sara Salih** with **Robert Young**

From issue 47 *Wasafiri* will be jointly published with Routledge.

Editorial	Subscriptions
Wasafiri Magazine	Taylor &Francis Customer Services
The Open University in London	Informa UK Ltd, Sheepen Place
1–11 Hawley Crescent	Colchester, Essex CO3 3LP
Camden Town	Telephone: 020 7017 5544 – general enquiries
London NW1 8NP	020 7017 5541 – agent enquiries
Email: wasafiri@open.ac.uk	Fax: 020 7017 5198
Telephone: 020 7556 6110	Email: tf.enquiries@tfinforma.com

www.wasafiri.org

MPT Subscription Form

Name	Address
Phone	Postcode
E-mail	Country

I would like to subscribe to *Modern Poetry in Translation* (please tick relevant box):

Subscription Rates (including postage by surface mail)

	UK	Overseas
❏ One year subscription (2 issues)	£22	£26 / US$ 48
❏ Two year subscription (4 issues) with discount	£40	£48 / US$ 88

Student Discount*

❏ One year subscription (2 issues)	£16	£20 / US$ 37
❏ Two year subscription (4 issues)	£28	£36 / US$ 66

Please indicate which year you expect to complete your studies 20 . . .

Standing Order Discount (only available to UK subscribers)

❏ Annual subscription (2 issues)	£20
❏ Student rate for annual subscription (2 issues)*	£14

Payment Method (please tick appropriate box)

❏ **Cheque:** please make cheques payable to: *Modern Poetry in Translation.* Sterling, US Dollar and Euro cheques accepted.

❏ **Standing Order:** please complete the standing order request below, indicating the date you would like your first payment to be taken. This should be at least one month after you return this form. We will set this up directly with your bank. Subsequent annual payments will be taken on the same date each year. For UK only.

Bank Name	Account Name
Branch Address	❏ Please notify my bank
	Please take my first payment on
Post Code	......./......./......... and future payments on
Sort Code	the same date each year.
Account Number	Signature:
	Date........./........./............

Bank Use Only: In favour of Modern Poetry in Translation, Lloyds TSB, 1 High St, Carfax, Oxford, OX1 4AA, UK a/c 03115155 Sort-code 30-96-35

Please return this form to The Administrator, MPT,
The Queen's College, Oxford, OX1 4AW, UK.
email queries to: administrator@mptmagazine.com